D0201577

Striking Thoughts

BRUCE LEE'S WISDOM
FOR DAILY LIVING

BY BRUCE LEE
Edited by John Little

The Bruce Lee Library

TUTTLE PUBLISHING
Tokyo • Rutland, Vermont • Singapore

Published by Tuttle Publishing, an imprint of Periplus Editions (HK) Ltd., with editorial offices at 364 Innovation Drive, North Clarendon, Vermont 05759 U.S.A.

Library of Congress Cataloging-in Publication Data

Lee, Bruce, 1940-1973
   Striking thoughts: Bruce Lee's wisdom for daily living / compiled and edited by
   John Little—1st ed.
         p. cm.
   I. Conduct of life. I. Little, John R., 1960- II. Title.
BJI581.2.L435 2000   99055240
191—dc21

ISBN 978-0-8048-3471-1

Distributed by

North America, Latin American & Europe
Tuttle Publishing
364 Innovation Drive
North Clarendon, VT 05759-9436 U.S.A.
Tel: 1 (802) 773-8930
Fax: 1 (802) 773-6993
info@tuttlepublishing.com
www.tuttlepublishing.com

Asia Pacific
Berkeley Books Pte. Ltd.
61 Tai Seng Avenue #02-12
Singapore 534167
Tel: (65) 6280-1330
Fax: (65) 6280-6290
inquiries@periplus.com.sg
www.periplus.com

Japan
Tuttle Publishing
Yaekari Building, 3rd Floor
5-4-12 Osaki, Shinagawa-ku
Tokyo 141 0032
Tel: (81) 3 5437-0171
Fax: (81) 3 5437-0755
tuttle-sales@gol.com

Indonesia
PT Java Books Indonesia
Kawasan Industri Pulogadung
Jl. Rawa Gelam IV No. 9
Jakarta 13930, Indonesia
Tel: (62-21) 4682-1088
Fax: (62-21) 461-0206
cs@javabooks.co.id

15 14 13 12 11 10 09   20 19 18 17 16 15 14 13 12
Text design— Dutton & Sherman
Printed in the United States of America

TUTTLE PUBLISHING ® is a registered trademark of Tuttle Publishing,
a division of Periplus Editions (HK) Ltd.

DEDICATION

To all men and women of every culture and

background who recognize with Bruce Lee that

"under the heavens there is but one family"—

and who dare to question those who would say otherwise.

It is your courage and your own "striking thoughts"

that will create a brighter future for us all.

CONTENTS

====================

PART II
On Being Human

PART III
On Matters of Existence

PART IV
On Achievement

PART V
On Art and Artists

PART VI
On Personal Liberation

PART VII
The Process of Becoming

PART VIII
On Ultimate (Final) Principles

RECOLLECTIONS ON THE THOUGHT OF BRUCE LEE

H E WAS A TEACHER first of all. He taught philosophy and tried to spread knowledge and wisdom. . . The integrity with which Bruce lived his life and tried to uphold what he believed to be right—that is a clear example of how it ought to be done. No matter what it is you're doing, do it with total honesty and total dedication. He definitely influenced me.

—Kareem Abdul-Jabbar

Bruce's philosophy seemed always to be going back to the Zen origins, where contradictory advice states the simplest of all truths. Bruce's lessons were lessons without being lessons; he was not a teacher, yet he was the greatest teacher I've ever known.

—Stirling Silliphant

For every question you asked him he would never have to think about it, he would just blurt it right out. Bruce would cover every point with a little saying. If he would see that you were having trouble with something, he would always know just what to tell you. It would seem like he was always dusting off your "bogie man." Like if there was something that you were scared of, Bruce would notice and then say, "Ah, scared of that, well look at it this way." He would change your whole idea about it. Bruce had sayings for everything.

—Bob Bremer, student of Bruce Lee

I thought Bruce was a brilliant, fine philosopher about everyday living. He was very much into finding out who he was. His comment to people was "Know yourself." The good head that he acquired was through his knowing himself. He and I used to have great long discussions about that. No matter what you do in life, if you don't know yourself, you're never going to be able to appreciate anything in life. That, I think, is today's mark of a good human being—to know yourself.

—Steve McQueen

We'd work out for an hour, then we'd talk for an hour about a lot things. He didn't separate life from the extension in his arm. And he is the only one I know of that carried it to the point of real art.

—James Coburn

P R E F A C E

The Philosophy of Bruce Lee

B RUCE LEE INSPIRED many people. Fans of his movies were dazzled by his physical brilliance, martial arts practitioners were awed by his deep understanding of the combative arts, while others found guidance in his underlying philosophy, which wove the spiritual and physical aspects of martial art together into a way of life.

His study of philosophy in college was the springboard of what would become a life-long exploration of the major thinkers of the world. He did not confine himself to any particular culture or philosophical era. Instead, he collected and avidly studied hundreds of books on all types of philosophy—Western, Eastern, ancient, and modern—in an attempt to glean those tenets that would contribute to his own spiritual growth.

Through the constant process of learning, Bruce evolved a personal philosophy, the central theme of which was the liberation of the spirit through greater self-knowledge. To free one's self from preconceived notions, prejudices, and conditioned responses is essential to understanding truth and reality. Martial art was the medium that gave Bruce the means to expand his potential and to share with others. As a teacher of the arts, Bruce had extraordinary talent. He often said, *"A teacher is never a giver of truth; he is a guide, a pointer to the truth that each student must find for himself. A good teacher is merely a catalyst."* One of his favorite stories that he would tell new students was the story of the "empty tea cup":

> A learned man once went to visit a Zen teacher to inquire about Zen. As the Zen teacher talked, the learned man frequently interrupted to express his own opinion about this or that.
>
> Finally, the Zen teacher stopped talking and began to serve tea to the learned man. He poured the cup full, then kept pouring until the cup overflowed.
>
> "Stop," said the learned man. "The cup is full, no more can be poured in."
>
> "Like this cup, you are full of your own opinions," replied the Zen teacher. "If you do not first empty your cup, how can you taste my cup of tea?"

Since he himself would not wholly accept any particular style of martial art or philosophy, Bruce encouraged his students not to accept, without question, his teachings. His main message was to keep one's mind, attitude, and senses pliable and receptive, and, at the same time, develop the ability to think critically. This process of inquiry, debate, and practice would lead not only to knowledge of one's physical strengths and weaknesses but also to the discovery of basic truths that allow one to grow toward a state of harmonious unity of spirit, mind, and body.

Bruce's teaching affected people in various ways. He often disturbed martial art practitioners by upsetting their set patterns of training and causing them to reconsider the blind acceptance of philosophical tenets. Those who studied with Bruce personally, or knew him through his writings, have been inspired to develop their potential beyond previously imposed limits, and to coordinate their minds and bodies to the point where confidence overrides fear.

By his example, Bruce encouraged his followers to be creative in directing their lives. "*Circumstances?*" he would say with a smile, "*Hell, I make circumstances!*" In his drive to realize his goals, Bruce refused to be hampered by adversity. His answer to problems was to turn a stumbling block into a stepping stone. For instance, when he was confined to bed rest for six months because of a back injury, he used that opportunity to compile his training methods and his philosophical thoughts into several volumes. [Editor's note: Apart from this volume, please see *Jeet Kune Do—Bruce Lee's Commentaries on the Martial Way* and *Bruce Lee—Artist of Life* in The Bruce Lee Library Series for many of these writings.]

Bruce Lee was a man born with a purpose who fulfilled a purpose much greater than even he had imagined.

The spirit of Bruce Lee continues to be the inspirational force that motivates young people to care for and nurture their bodies and souls and to bring out the best that they have within themselves. As many fans have commented— "Bruce Lee made a difference in my life."

— *Linda Lee Cadwell*

INTRODUCTION

A Book For
Free Spirits

*Self-actualization is the important thing. And my
personal message to people is that I hope they will
go toward self-actualization rather than self-image
actualization. I hope that they will search within
themselves for honest self-expression.*

—*Bruce Lee*

Bruce Lee changed worlds—the world of martial
arts, the worlds of Asian and American cinema,
and the personal worlds of countless students and
fans have been transformed by his brilliance. Far more
than just a passing influence, Lee has continued to
inspire and stimulate the minds of individuals from all
walks of life for decades. Interest in his thought is on the
rise and many regard him as a contemporary philosopher
and visionary, discovering in his words an antidote to *con-*

temporary problems, as well as finding him a model of discipline, strength, and wisdom. Lee's philosophy forms for us a vision of a world of progress, a world free of suffering, and a world of enlightenment unflawed by ignorance, superstition, and corruption. In Lee's words, a world of *"love, peace and brotherhood."*

To Bruce Lee, philosophy was not the professional playground of academics, but every human being's gateway to the greatest adventure of the human spirit. It illuminated the frontiers of human possibility and obliterated the shadows of doubt and insecurity. Unlike others, content to follow, Bruce Lee insisted upon charting his own course toward truth, and he encouraged those who wished to share his insights to do likewise. While Lee was a champion of individual rights and individual development, both of which stress the sovereignty of the individual as an end in himself, he also spoke to something deeper—the commonality of all human beings and the removal of such artificial barriers to true brotherhood as nationality, ethnicity, and class structure, so that human beings could live together peaceably as independent equals.

Bruce Lee rejected blind obedience to external authority. He urged human beings to hold themselves and their lives as their highest values and wrote in praise of "the artist of life" who lives by his own judgment and who is willing to stand alone against tradition and popular opinion. Lee pointed out that *"We have more faith in what we imitate than in what we originate,"* with the result that we are encouraged—and have opted—to look to anyone but ourselves for the answers to our most unsettling questions. Too many are confused about whom to trust, suspicious of their own impulses and uncertain of their futures. Spirits have been malnourished and minds stunted by allowing others to "take over" or decide what constitute "real" problems.

Striking Thoughts: Bruce Lee's Wisdom for Daily Living, then, is a book for the free spirit who chooses to live by the power of his or her own mind rather than relying on the dictates of creed or institution in making decisions about life and how to live it. Consisting of eight sections, 72 topics, and 825 aphorisms, *Striking Thoughts* is for all who have sought truth but not found it in platitude or dogma. Within the pages of *Striking Thoughts* you will find that Bruce Lee has not so much prepared a banquet of easy answers as outlined a means by which you can prepare your own way. And if you are suffering, dispirited, or anxious, in his words you will find observations and insights that can fortify you and pacify your troubled spirit.

How can I say such things? Simply because Bruce Lee's words have done as much for me—and for thousands more from all walks of life and from all over the world who have taken the time to write or e-mail The Bruce Lee Educational Foundation offering identical testimony. It is easy to see the appeal of Lee's thought, for he dares to say that which others dare only to think; his candor disarms our insecurities and fears. Lee is capable of infusing a single sentence with a profundity that would take others at least a chapter to convey; his every aphorism is a mountain peak, offering a higher vantage point for viewing the unfolding of life's means and mysteries. The supreme irony is that this profound thought was the fruit of a life that spanned a mere 32 years.

The title "Striking Thoughts" is taken from a heading that Bruce Lee created for a series of maxims he wrote down after reading the philosopher Jiddu Krishnamurti's book *First and Last Freedom*. However, the committing to paper (and, later, to audiotape) of "striking thoughts" was a habit of Lee's that extended back to his early days in Hong Kong. Included within the pages of this book are those "striking thoughts" that issued forth in conversations, interviews, and correspondence that Bruce Lee shared with journalists, friends, and colleagues. Other entries are postulates that Lee had been moved to type out—perhaps with an eye toward one day making use of them—others were quickly jotted down before they escaped his concentration. Still others were noted in book margins as he read; the result of a "striking thought" that had come to him as he was closely regarding a particular writer or philosopher's point of view.

Lee's personal library contained the works of many great and diverse philosophers and sages from many different cultures and provided him with a broad comprehension of how all people—as opposed to only people from his own personal experience—actually viewed life, with its joy and suffering. Their varying viewpoints served as just instrument, too, for such a man as Bruce Lee, who wished to exercise the varied possibilities of speculation, who cared to clarify his own mind rather than to put forth finalities when life itself was so blind and inconclusive. After all, a dogmatic conclusion, Lee believed, was all too often merely the point at which the sails of thought had lost their wind.

Bruce Lee's most common educational and literary form was the aphorism, and this presentation follows that style. This book could be read like Bartlett's *Familiar Quotations*, but what one ultimately gets out of Bruce Lee will be directly proportionate to the sustained attention one accords him. It was always the individual whom Lee chose to address and it must be remembered that he wrote primarily to express his own personal feelings on life, rather than to be read as a dogmatic arsenal of arguments for or against something. Lee grasped the point that in the realm of philosophy "less is more," and it's precisely for this reason that Lee's writings—particularly his aphorisms—gracefully transcend the plodding complexity of traditional philosophy and serve a breath of fresh air to those accustomed to taking their philosophical medicine with heavy doses of metaphysics and epistemology. The intent of the aphorism is to arouse a heartfelt "call to arms" and not intellectual abstraction—however valid such abstraction may prove to be. As Lee himself says in one of his aphorisms:

The end of man is action and not thought, though it be of the noblest.

Bruce Lee's use of aphorism generally consists of starting with a familiar and important aspect of life, then positioning it to awaken people to the problems inherent in the conventional assumptions made on the topic. The result of Lee's statement is that the reader is now compelled to think for himself about the issue, which leads the individual to produce his *own* answer. Lee always challenged his students (both in the classroom and through his writings) not to agree or disagree—but to *grow*.

Lee's constant questioning—of himself as well as of assumed truth—more often than not reveals to us the inadequacy of the conventional position on such matters. It's this questioning that provides the necessary basis for real understanding to occur. As Lee himself said, it is only *"in the contrast of comparison some new thing might grow."* Lee was firmly insistent that even if he were to know the answers, and even if he were to tell them to us, they wouldn't do us any good. In other words, it's in the nature of Lee's statements on life that you have to puzzle out their validity for yourself. To Lee's way of thinking, any answer he could provide is worth nothing to any other individual, unless that individual has come to see its validity as result of his own independent thought on the matter. This is why Lee's philosophical writings are so successful as instruments for drawing you into your own mind and, by extension, into the realm of philosophy.

The processes of search and inquiry are important, but they must be followed with an alert understanding that—because our assumptions and beliefs are in fact open to perpetual questioning—our "conclusions" don't hold any special or privileged status. They are merely staging posts on the road to further inquiries we must continue to make throughout our lives. Recognizing that his own positions on such issues could easily be made dogma by his students, Lee instead chose to deploy the Socratic method of challenging his students (and now the reader) to confront or address, from within, the problems of existence that were besetting them. Lee held that if there is a "way" then it most assuredly is somebody else's—not yours—with the result that following it would lead you further away from the truth that resides within you. It is for this reason, as Lee indicates below, that it is imperative that the free spirit not mistake any book—including this one—or its contents for the truth, for then it will simply become yet another external authority:

> *Independent inquiry is needed in your search for truth, not dependence on anyone else's view or a mere book.*

Or, as Lee cautioned in his last film, *Enter the Dragon*:

> *It is like a finger pointing a way to the moon. Don't concentrate on the finger or you will miss all that heavenly glory.*

The objective of this volume, then, is two-fold; to have Bruce Lee communicate with you and to have you communicate with yourself. This counsel given by Lee with regard to his teachings is particularly pertinent:

> *To live is a constant process of relating, so come on out of that shell of isolation and conclusion, and relate DIRECTLY to what is being said. Bear in mind I seek neither your approval nor to influence you. So do not make up your mind as to "this is this" or "that is that." I will be more than satisfied if you begin to learn to investigate everything yourself from now on.*

What Bruce Lee communicates to you in these pages is for you alone to interpret, and it falls solely to you to make of it what you will.

—*John Little*

Independent inquiry is needed in your search for truth,
not dependence on anyone else's view or a mere book.

—*Bruce Lee*

PART ONE

On First Principles

Life

Emptiness the starting point. — In order to taste my cup of water you must first empty your cup. My friend, drop all of your preconceived fixed ideas and be neutral. Do you know why this cup is so useful? Because it is *empty*.

Flow in the process of life. — You can never step in the same water twice, my friend. Like flowing water, life is perpetual movement. There is nothing fixed. Whatever your problems happen to be in the future, remember well that they cannot remain stationary but must move together with your living spirit. Otherwise, you will drift into artificiality or attempt to solidify the ever-flowing. To avoid that, you must change and be flexible. Remember, the usefulness of a cup is in its emptiness.

Life has no frontier. — Life is wide, limitless. There is no border, no frontier.

To live is a constant process of relating. — To live is a constant process of relating, so come on out of that shell of isolation and conclusion, and relate DIRECTLY to what is being said. Bear in mind I seek neither your approval nor to influence you. So do not make up your mind as to "this is this" or "that is that." I will be more than satisfied if you begin to learn to investigate everything yourself from now on.

Life simply is. — Living exists when life lives through us — unhampered in its flow, for he who is living is not conscious of living and, in this, is the life it lives. Life lives; and in the living flow, no questions are raised. The reason is that life is a living now! So, in order to live life wholeheartedly, the answer is life simply *is*.

Life — for its own sake. — Realize the fact that you simply "live" and not "live for."

The meaning of life. — The meaning of life is that it is to be *lived,* and it is not to be traded and conceptualized and squeezed into a pattern of systems.

Life is the effect of feelings. — Life is simply what our feelings do to us.

The meaning in life. — All in all, the goal of my planning and doing is to find the true meaning in life — peace of mind. In order to achieve this peace of mind, the teaching of detachment of Taoism and Zen proved to be valuable.

The secret of life. — The aphorism "as a man thinketh in his heart so is he"* contains the secret of life. James Allen further added "A man is literally what he thinks." This might be a shocking statement, but everything is a state of mind.

Meaning is found in relationship. — Meaning is the relationship of the foreground figure to the background.

Manipulation and control are not the ultimate joy of life. — We realize that manipulation and control are not the ultimate joy of life — to become real, to learn to take a stand, to develop one's center, to the support of our total personality, a release to spontaneity — yes, yes, yes!

The essence of life. — The essence: free movement of spirit. Original essence.

Violence is a part of life. — It should be remembered that violence and aggression is part of everyday life now. You see it over the TV. You can't just pretend that it does not exist.

* Note: This is also found in Proverbs 23:7 which says "As he thinketh in his heart, so is he."

The principle of life. — Life is never stagnation. It is a constant movement, unrhythmic movement, as well as constant change. Things live by moving and gain strength as they go.

Life is sometimes unpleasant. — Life is an ever-flowing process and somewhere on the path some unpleasant things will pop up — it might leave a scar, but then life is flowing, and like running water, when it stops it grows stale. Go bravely on, my friend, because each experience teaches us a lesson. Keep blasting because life is such that sometimes it is nice and sometimes it is not.

The pendulum of life must have balance. — Only sober moderation lasts, and that persists through all time. Only the midpart of anything is preserved because the pendulum of life must have balance, and the midpart is the balance.

Pliability is life. — Be pliable. When a man is living, he is soft and pliable; when he is dead, he becomes rigid. Pliability is life; rigidity is death, whether one speaks of man's body, his mind, or his spirit.

Life as educator. — Life itself is your teacher, and you are in a state of constant learning.

To live is to create. — To live is to express, and to express you have to create. Creation is never merely repetition. To live is to express oneself freely in creation.

The process of life. — Since life is an ever-evolving process, one should flow in this process and discover how to actualize and expand oneself.

The oneness of life. — The oneness of all life is a truth that can be fully realized only when false notions of a separate self — whose destiny can be considered apart from the WHOLE — are forever annihilated.

The life of perfection is the simple life. — A simple life is one of plainness, in which profit is discarded, cleverness abandoned, selfishness eliminated, and desires reduced. It is the life of perfection which seems to be incomplete, and of fullness which seems to be empty. It is the life which is as bright as light, but does not dazzle. In short, it is a life of harmony, unity, contentment, tranquillity, constancy, enlightenment, peace, and long life.

Life must be understood from moment to moment. — Life is something for which there is no answer; it must be understood from moment to moment — the answer we find inevitably conforms to the pattern of what we think we know.

Enjoy yourself. — Remember my friend to enjoy your planning as well as your accomplishment, for life is too short for negative energy.

Existence

Existence and anti-existence. — What is the opposite of existence? The immediate answer would be "nonexistence," but this is incorrect. The opposite would be anti-existence, just as the opposite of matter is antimatter.

Existence precedes consciousness. — The primary reality is not what I think, but that I live, for those also live who do not think. Although this living may not be a real living. God! What contradictions when we seek to join in wedlock life and reason!

Existence is dynamic. — This state is far from static, it is a being without continuity.

"Sum, ergo cogito." — The truth is "Sum, ergo cogito;" "I am, therefore I think," although not everything that is thinks. Is not conscious thinking above all consciousness of being? Is pure thought possible, without consciousness of self, without personality? Can there exist pure knowledge without feeling, without that species of materiality which feeling lends to it? Do we not perhaps feel thought, and do we not feel ourselves in the act of knowing and willing?

The fundamental relationship between existence and cognition. — To doubt is to think, and thought is the only thing in the universe whose existence cannot be denied, because to deny is to think. When one says that thought exists, it automatically includes saying that one exists because there is no thought that does not contain as one of its elements a subject who thinks.

Time

On past, present, and future. — My friend, do think of the past in terms of those memories of events and accomplishments which were pleasant, rewarding, and satisfying. The present? Well, think of it in terms of challenges and opportunities, and the rewards available for the application of your talents and energies. As for the future, that is a time and a place where every worthy ambition you possess is within your grasp.

The timeless moment. — The "moment" has no yesterday or tomorrow. It is not the result of thought and therefore has no time.

Knowledge, knowing, and time. — Knowledge, surely, is always of time, whereas knowing is not of time. Knowledge is from a source, from an accumulation, from a conclusion, while knowing is a movement.

To be free of the bonds of time. — To realize freedom the mind has to learn to look at life, which is vast movement, without the bondage of time, for freedom lies beyond the field of consciousness — care for watching, but don't stop and interpret "I am free," then you're living in a memory of something that has gone.

Time spent vs. time wasted. — To spend time is to pass it in a specified manner. To waste time is to expend it thoughtlessly or carelessly. We all have time to either spend or waste, and it is our decision what to do with it. But once passed, it is gone forever.

The value of time. — Time means a lot to me because, you see, I, too, am also a learner and am often lost in the joy of forever developing and simplifying. If you love life, don't waste time, for time is what life is made up of.

Time and philosophy. — My only problem these days is time. I find myself dashing back and forth between Los Angeles and Hong Kong four and five times a year. It is a very schizophrenic way to make a living, but then, that's what University of Washington philosophy courses prepare you for, I suppose.

The Root

The root in life. — Be aware of doing your best to understand the ROOT in life and realize the DIRECT and the INDIRECT are in fact a complementary WHOLE. It is to see things as they are and not to become attached to anything — to be unconscious means to be innocent of the working of a relative (empirical) mind — when there is no abiding of thought anywhere on anything — this is being unbound. This not abiding anywhere is the root of our life.

The root of concentration. — Concentration is the ROOT of all the higher abilities in man.

Seek to understand the root. — It is futile to argue as to which single leaf, which design of branch, or which attractive flower you like; when you understand the root, you understand all its blossoming.

The root vs. the branches. — What we are after is the ROOT and not the branches. The root is the real knowledge; the branches are surface knowledge. Real knowledge breeds "body feel" and personal expression; surface knowledge breeds mechanical conditioning and imposing limitation and squelches creativity.

Express your total presence from the root. — Be at once absorbingly open and rootily relaying your captivating total presence with appropriate inward time.

The root is the starting point. — The root is the fulcrum on which will rest the expression of your soul; the root is the "starting point" of all natural manifestation. If the root is right so will be all its manifestation. It cannot be, when the root is neglected, that what should spring from it will be well-ordered.

The Now

The Now is truth. — This evening I see something totally new, and that newness is experienced by the mind; but tomorrow that experience becomes mechanical, because I want to repeat the sensation, the pleasure of it — the description is never real. What is real is seeing the truth instantaneously, because truth has no future.

The Now is all-inclusive. — NOTHING EXISTS EXCEPT THE HERE AND NOW.

The Now covers all that exists. — The part is no more, the future is not yet. NOW includes the balance of being here, experiencing, involvement, phenomenon, awareness.

Flow in the living moment. — We are always in a process of becoming and NOTHING is fixed. Have no rigid system in you, and you'll be flexible to change with the ever changing. OPEN yourself and flow, my friend. Flow in the TOTAL OPENESS OF THE LIVING MOMENT. If nothing within you stays rigid, outward things will disclose themselves. Moving, be like water. Still, be like a mirror. Respond like an echo.

The Now is total awareness. — The "space" created between "what is" and "what should be." Total awareness of the now and not the disciplined stillness.

You cannot force the Now. — But can you neither condemn nor justify and yet be extraordinarily alive as you walk on? You can never invite the wind, but you must leave the window open.

Being in the Now. — Listen. Can you hear the wind? And can you hear the birds singing? You have to HEAR IT. Empty your mind. You know how water fills a cup? It BECOMES that cup. You have to think about nothing. You have to BECOME nothing.

The Moment is freedom. — I couldn't live by a rigid schedule. I try to live freely from moment to moment, letting things happen and adjusting to them.

The Now is creative. — If you are in the *NOW*, you are creative.

The Now is inventive. — If you are in the NOW, you are inventive.

There is no anxiety in the Now. — When you are in the NOW, you can't be anxious, because the excitement flows immediately into ongoing spontaneous activity.

The Now and its synonyms. — One and the same thing:

· Living in the NOW

· Maturity

· Authenticity

· Responsibility for one's action/life

· Response — Ability

· Having the Creativeness of the NOW available

To live now you must die to yesterday. — To understand and live now, there must be dying to everything of yesterday. Die continually to every newly gained experience—be in a state of choiceless awareness of WHAT IS.

The Now is indivisible. — Completeness, the now, is an absence of the conscious mind to strive to divide that which is indivisible. For once the completeness of things is taken apart, it is no longer complete. All the pieces of a car that has been taken apart may be there, but it is no longer a car in its original nature, which is its function or life.

Reality

Matter and energy are one. — In atomic physics no distinction is recognized between matter and energy; nor is it possible to make such a distinction, since they are in reality one essence, or at least two poles of the same unit. It is no longer possible, as it was in the mechanistic scientific era, to absolutely define weight, length, or time, etc., as the work of Einstein, Plank, Whitehead, and Jeans has demonstrated.

Reality: the Western approach. — The Western approach to reality is mostly through theory, and theory begins by denying reality — to talk about reality, to go around reality, to catch anything that attracts our sense — intellect and abstract it away from reality itself.

No-thingness is a form of process. — In science we have finally come back to the pre-Socratic philosopher, Heraclitus, who said that everything is flow, flux, process. There are no "things." NOTHINGNESS in Eastern language is "no-thingness." We in the West think of nothingness as a void, an emptiness, a nonexistence. In Eastern philosophy and modern physical science, nothingness — no-thingness — is a form of process, ever moving.

"Is" vs. "should." What is and what should be. — What IS is more important than WHAT SHOULD BE. Too many people are looking at "what is" from a position of thinking "what should be."

Western philosophy's denial of reality. — The Western approach to reality is mostly through theory, and theory begins by denying reality — to talk about reality, to go around reality, to catch anything that attracts our sense — intellect and abstract it away form reality itself. Thus philosophy begins by saying that the outside world is not a basic fact, that its existence can be doubted and that every proposition in which the reality of the outside world is affirmed is not an evident proposition but one that needs to be divided, dissected, and analyzed. It is to stand consciously aside and try to square a circle.

There is no method to reality. — Do not reduce reality to a static thing and then invent methods by which to reach it.

Reality and perception. — There is a difference:

- · The world

- · Our reaction to it

Experiencing is believing. — A fat belly cannot believe that such a thing as hunger exists.

Be arduous in locating "this." — While walking or resting, sitting or lying, while talking or remaining. . . quiet, while eating or drinking, do not allow yourself to be indolent, but be most arduous in search of "THIS."

The formal reality of a thing. — Whatever exists has certain reality. Nonrepresentation of an object is not a formal reality.

On causality. — Everything has to have a cause.

Reality and the law of cause and effect. — The cause must have the same reality as the effect.

Commonality of all physical objects. — All physical objects are the same. Therefore, the knowledge of knowing the existence of a physical object is enough.

Formal reality equals objective reality. — There must be more or as much formal reality as objective reality.

Matter and the need for security. — In science we try to find ultimate matter, but the more we split up matter, the more we find other matter. We find movement, and movement equals energy: movement, impact, energy, but no things. Things came about, more or less, by man's need for security. You can manipulate a thing, you can play fitting games with it. These concepts, these somethings can be put together into something else. "Something" is a thing, so even an abstract noun becomes a thing.

Calm your mind to really see. — At this moment stop inwardly — when you do stop inwardly, psychologically, your mind becomes very peaceful, very clear. Then you can really look at "this."

Remove the dirt of preconceived opinion. — Scratch away all the dirt our being has accumulated and reveal reality in its *is-ness*, or in its suchness, or in its nakedness, which corresponds to the Buddhist concept of emptiness.

Conditioning obstructs our view of reality. — We do not see *IT* in its suchness because of our indoctrination, crooked and twisted.

True thusness and thought. — True thusness is without defiling thought; it cannot be known through conception and thought.

Reality is apparent when one ceases to compare. — There is "what is" only when there is no comparison at all, and to live with what is, is to be peaceful.

Reality is being itself. — It is being itself, in becoming itself. Reality in its isness, the "isness" of a thing. Thus isness is the meaning — having freedom in its primary sense — not limited by attachments, confinements, partialization, complexities.

The Laws

The law of self-will. — A self-willed man obeys a different law, the one law I, too, hold absolutely sacred — the human law in himself, his own individual will.

The law of cause and effect. — Every circumstance of every man's life is the result of a definite cause — mode and control are yours.

The law of identity. — The law of identity states that "A is A." This means that every logical statement is either true or false but that no statement is both true and false in the same context.

The law of harmony. — The law of harmony, in which one should be in harmony with, and not in opposition to, the strength and force of the opposition. This means that one should do nothing that is not natural or spontaneous; the important thing is not to strain in any way.

The law of non-interference with nature. — The law of non-interference with nature is a basic principle of Taoism [stating] that one should be in harmony with, not rebellion against, the fundamental laws of the universe. Preserve yourself by following the natural bends of things and don't interfere. Remember never to assert your self against nature; never be in frontal opposition to any problems, but to control it by swinging with it.

Interdependency

Dualism vs. monism. — The dualistic philosophy reigned supreme in Europe, dominating the development of Western science. But with the advent of atomic physics, findings based on demonstrable experiment were seen to negate the dualistic theory, and the trend of thought since then has been back toward the monistic conception of the ancient Taoists.

The interdependency of thought and existence. — If thought exists, I who think and the world about which I think also exist; the one exists but for the other, having no possible separation between them. Therefore, the world and I are both in active correlation; I am that which sees the world, and the world is that which is seen by me. I exist for the world, and the world exists for me. If there were no things to be seen, thought about, and imagined, I would not see, think, or imagine. That is to say, I would not exist. One sure and primary and fundamental fact is the joint existence of a subject and of its world. The one does not exist without the other. I acquire no understanding of myself except as I take account of objects, of the surroundings. I do not think unless I think of things — and there I find myself.

The relationship of subject and object. — It is of no use to talk merely about objects of consciousness, whether they are thought sensations or wax candles. An object must have a subject, and subject-object is a pair of complementaries (not opposites), like all others, which are two halves of one whole, and are a function each of the other. When we hold to the core, the opposite sides are the same if they are seen from the center of the moving circle. I do not experience; I am experience. I am not the subject of an experience; I am that experience. I am awareness. Nothing else can be I or can exist.

The subject/object relationship and "the-moon-in-the-water." — The phenomenon of moon-in-the-water is likened to human experience. The water is the subject, and the moon the object. When there is no water, there is no moon-in-the-water, and likewise when there is no moon. But when the moon rises, the water does not wait to receive its image, and when even the tiniest drop of water is poured out, the moon does not wait to cast its reflection. For the moon does not intend to cast its reflection, and the water does not receive its image on purpose. The event is caused as much by the water as by the moon, and as the water manifests the brightness of the moon, the moon manifests the clarity of the water.

Interdependency and Taoism. — Taoist philosophy, against the background of which acupuncture had its origin and developed, is essentially monistic. The Chinese conceived the entire universe as activated by two principles, the Yang and the Yin, the positive and negative, and they considered that nothing that exists, either animate or so-called inanimate, does so except by virtue of the ceaseless interplay of these two forces. Matter and energy, Yang and Yin, heaven and earth, are conceived of as essentially one or as two coexistent poles of one indivisible whole.

The Void

On voidness. — Voidness is that which stands right in the middle between this and that. The void is all-inclusive; having no opposite, there is nothing which it excludes or opposes. The all-illuminating light shines and is beyond the movement of the opposites.

The living void. — It is living void, because all forms come out of it, and whoever realizes the void is filled with life and power and the love of all beings.

The void as creative energy. — The primordial creative energy affects the whole person and not a mere fragment — it is creation uncontaminated by thought; the creative tide in us that flows outward.

The void and nothingness. — NOTHINGNESS means "no thingness" — there is only process, happening. When we ACCEPT and ENTER this nothingness, the void, then the desert starts to bloom. The empty void becomes alive, IS BEING FILLED. The sterile void becomes the fertile void. I am nothing but function. Nothing equals real.

The two aspects of the void. — The void (or the unconscious) may be said to have two aspects:

· It simply is what it is.

· It is realized, it is aware of itself, and to speak improperly, this awareness is "in us," or better, we are "in it."

The ultimate transcends human understanding ("no-abode"). — The ultimate source of all things is beyond human understanding, beyond the categories of time and space. As it thus transcends all modes of relativity, it is called "having no abode" to which any possible predications are applicable.

On Death

Don't neglect life by worrying about death. — I don't know what is the meaning of death, but I am not afraid to die — and I go on, non-stop, going forward [with life]. Even though I, Bruce Lee, may die some day without fulfilling all of my ambitions, I will have no regrets. I did what I wanted to do and what I've done, I've done with sincerity and to the best of my ability. You can't expect much more from life.

The way of death. — Through the ages, the end for heroes is the same as for ordinary men. They all died and gradually faded away in the memory of man.

Acceptance of death. — The round of summer and winter becomes a blessing the moment we give up the fantasy of eternal spring.

The art of dying. — Like everyone else, you want to learn the way to win. But never to accept the way to lose. To accept defeat — to learn to die — is be liberated from it. Once you accept, you are free to flow and to harmonize. Fluidity is the way to an empty mind. You must free your ambitious mind and learn the art of dying.

On separating from dear friends. — Here now, forever more our lives must part. My path leads there and yours another way; I know not where tomorrow's path may lead, nor what the future holds.

On the need to remember. — Remembrance is the only paradise out of which we cannot be driven away. Pleasure is the flower that fades, remembrance is the lasting perfume. Remembrances last longer than present realities; I have preserved blossoms for many years, but never fruits.

PART TWO

On Being
Human

The Human Being

Identify with your humanity. — You know how I like to think of myself? As a human being.

The function and duty of a human being. — The function and duty of a human being, a "quality" human being, that is, is the sincere and honest development of potential and self-actualization. One additional comment: the energy from within and the physical strength from your body can guide you toward accomplishing your purpose in life — and to actually act on actualizing your duty to yourself.

Human beings are integrators. — We do not analyze. We IN-TEGRATE.

The goal of a human being. — The human goal: to actualize oneself.

False people. — What I detest most are dishonest people who talk more than they are capable of doing and also people who use false humility as a means to cover their obnoxious inadequacy.

On the Dominican Republic. — I like the country and the people. The Dominicans have the simplicity of a real human being; there is not so much hypocrisy like in the big cities.

On the nature of human beings. — A human being is an eating, sleeping, physically maintaining, reproducing entity. A human being is an entity of feeling. A human being is a creating entity.

A human being is the result of a marriage of natural instinct and control. — Here is natural instinct, and there is control. You are to combine the two in harmony. If you have one to the extreme you will be very unscientific; if you have another to the extreme, you become a mechanical man, no longer a human being. So it is a successful combination of both. It is not pure naturalness, or pure unnaturalness. The ideal is unnatural naturalness or natural unnaturalness.

A human being is the creative animal. — It is the creative ability of a human being that separates him from all other animals.

On developing human potential. — To promote the growth process and develop human potential:

- To get through social role playing
- To fill in the holes in the personality to make [one] whole and complete again.

We are capable of much more. — The fact [is] that we live only on such a small percentage of our potential:

- You do not allow yourself to be totally yourself
- Society does not allow you to be totally yourself.

Talking and listening. — Most people can talk without listening. Very few can listen without talking. It is very rare that people can talk and listen.

The fundamental moral question for human beings. — What is the right (i.e., just, ethical, moral) conduct for a human being?

Self-honesty leads to one becoming a "real" human being. — What the hell; you are what you are, and self-honesty occupies a definite and vital part in the ever-growing process to become a "real" human being and not a plastic one. Somehow, one day, you will hear *"hey, now that's quality; here is someone REAL."* I'd like that.

Action

The necessity for acting on our beliefs. — Knowing is not enough; we must apply. Willing is not enough; we must do.

Action is a highroad to self-esteem. — Action is a highroad to self-confidence and esteem. Where it is open, all energies flow toward it. It comes readily to most people, and its rewards are tangible.

Only actions give life strength. — Only actions give to life its strength, as only moderation gives it its charm.

Not to think, but to do. — Our grand business is not to see what lies dimly at a distance, but to do what lies clearly at hand.

The point is the doing. — The point is the doing of them rather than the accomplishments. There is no actor but the action — there is no experiencer but experience.

The end of man is action. — The end of man is action, and not thought, though it be of the noblest. In this world there are a lot of people who cannot touch the heart of the matter but talk merely intellectually (not emotionally) about how they would do this or do that; talk about it, but yet nothing is ever actualized or accomplished.

The reward of doing. — The doer alone learns.

There is action mentally and physically. — Mental "motion" is present with every physical action.

Wu-wei (natural action)

Wu-wei is natural action. — The basic idea of the *Tao Te Ching* is NATURALISM in the sense of wu-wei (inaction), which really means taking no unnatural action. It means spontaneity; that is, "to support all things in their natural stage" and thus allow them to "transform spontaneously." In this manner Tao "Undertakes no activity and yet there is nothing left undone."

Wu-wei's expression in daily life. — In ordinary life wu-wei is expressed in "producing and rearing things without taking possession of them" and "doing work but not taking pride in it" — thus the natural "way" stands in complement to all artificial ways such as regulation, ceremonies, etc. This is the reason why the Taoists don't like formalities and artificialities.

On not expending one's powers prematurely. — The work of conservation is shown to be a continuous actualization and differentiation of form. One does not allow oneself to be influenced by outward success or failure, but confident in one's strength, one bides one's time.

You do not need special training. — There is no need to exert oneself in special cultivation outside the daily round of living.

Do not expend power prematurely. — Wait in the calm strength of patience — he that is strong should guard it with tenderness. One need not fear lest strong will should not prevail; the main thing is not to expend one's powers prematurely in an attempt to obtain by force something for which the time is not yet ripe.

Natural action is pliable. — Non-action, as it is often translated, does not mean no action, but no such action as begets opposition. "Right" action is neither to oppose nor to give way, but to be pliable, as a reed in the wind.

Wu-wei is spontaneous action. — Spontaneous action — of which Nature (Tao) was the grand practitioner. This action of Nature was real action. The second was action taken with design, premeditated, and directed to chosen ends. This, however attractive it might seem, was a forcing of Nature and therefore unreal.

Action in conformity with the situation. — The person is[[in?]] question is not in an independent position, but is acting as an assistant. It is not his task to try to lead — that would only make him lose the Way — but to let himself be led. If he knows how to meet fate with an attitude of acceptance, he is sure to find the right guidance. The superior man lets himself be guided; he does not go ahead blindly, but learns from the situation what is demanded of him and then follows.

Don't seek, but allow. — Do not seek IT, for it will come when least expected. Let go. Don't seek or run away.

On the principle of wu-wei. — Wu-wei is spontaneous superiority. Wu-wei is spontaneous action without prearrangement. Wu-wei ensures the spirit of harmony with nature. Wu-wei sees no violence done, with the result of peace and freedom from disturbance. Wu-wei is the nourishment of the spirit, left alone, so it can find stability. Wu-wei is "taking no action;" all effort made with a purpose are sure to fail.

Wu-wei is creative intuition. — The principle of wu-wei is entirely anaction of creative intuition, which opens the well-springs WITHIN man. While the action of assertion, man's common tendency, is preconceptual and rational, it cannot penetrate the hidden recesses of creativity. The action of assertion is viewed from the externals of intellection, while the action of non-assertion is activated by the inner light. The former action is limited and finite, the latter free and limitless.

The Mind

An intelligent mind is constantly learning. — An intelligent mind is one which is constantly learning, never concluding — styles and patterns have come to conclusion, therefore they [have] ceased to be intelligent.

An intelligent mind is an inquiring mind. — An intelligent mind is an INQUIRING mind. It is not satisfied with explanations, with conclusions; nor is it a mind that believes, because belief is again another form of conclusion.

The qualities of mind. — To be one thing and not to change is the climax of STILLNESS. To have nothing in one that resists is the climax of EMPTINESS. To remain detached from all outside things is the climax of FINENESS. To have in oneself no contraries is the climax of PURITY.

You are the commander of your mind. — I've always been buffeted by circumstances because I thought of myself as a human being [affected by] outside conditioning. Now I realize that I am the power that commands the feeling of my mind and from which circumstances grow.

On the value of keeping an open mind. — The usefulness of a cup is in its emptiness. Emptiness = Totality. Totality of mind; totality of physical structure.

To free the mind. — In order that the mind may function naturally and harmoniously it must be freed from all attachment to oppositional notions. The mind should be freed from the influence of the external world. To let the mind take its course unhindered among phenomena. Not the cultivated innocence of a clever mind that wants to be innocent, but that state of innocence in which there is no denial or acceptance, and in which the mind just sees what is.

All thought is partial. — All thought is partial, it can never be total. Thought is the response of memory, and memory is always partial, because memory is the result of experience; so thought is the reaction of a mind which is conditioned by experience

A limited mind cannot think freely. — The mind must be wide open in order to function freely in thought. For a limited mind cannot think freely.

The mind responds. — The waters are in motion all the time, but the moon retains its serenity. The mind moves in response to the ten thousand situations but remains ever the same.

Don't be a slave to learning. — Learning is important but do not become its slave. Above all, do not harbor anything external and superfluous, the mind is the primary.

Seeing takes place with the inner mind. — Sharpen the psychic power of seeing in order to act immediately in accordance with what it sees — the seeing takes place with the inner mind.

The mind is an ultimate reality. — Mind is an ultimate reality which is aware of itself and is not the seat of our empirical consciousness — by "being" mind instead of "having" mind.

Mind is the dynamic aspect of emptiness. — All movements come out of emptiness and that the mind is the name given to this dynamic aspect of emptiness, and further that here is no crookedness, no ego-centered motivation, as the emptiness is sincerity, genuineness, and straightforwardness allowing nothing between itself and its movements.

Don't direct the mind. — Stand at the neutral point between negative and positive, no longer directing one's mind to anything.

The mind is without activity. — The mind is originally without activity; the Way is always without thought.

The unconditioned mind intuits truth. — [To] bring the mind into sharp focus and to make it alert so that it can immediately intuit truth, which is everywhere, the mind must be emancipated from old habits, prejudices, restrictive thought process, and even ordinary thought itself.

Cultivate an alert mind. — To be on the alert means to be deadly serious; to be deadly serious means to be sincere to oneself, and it is sincerity that finally leads to the *Way*.

Knowledge is of the mind. — By knowledge is meant knowing the emptiness and tranquillity of the mind. Insight means realizing the one's original nature is not created.

Knowledge is of the past. — Knowledge is of the past; learning is in the present, a constant movement, in relationship with the outward things, without the past.

The infinite mobilities of the mind. — The mind itself is endowed with infinite mobilities that know no hindrances.

The rectified mind. — A rectified mind is a mind immune to emotional influences — free from fear, anger, sorrow, anxiety, and even fond attachment — when the mind is not present, we look and do not see; we hear and do not understand; we eat and do not know the taste of what we eat.

Thinking

Sincere thought. — Sincere thought means thought of concentration (quiet awareness). The thought of a distracted mind cannot be sincere.

Inner thought and outer expression are one. — Man's mind and his behavior are one, his inner thought and outer expression cannot contradict each other. Therefore a man should set up his right principle, and this right mind (principle) will influence his action.

Learning is never cumulative. — The additive process is merely a cultivation of memory, which becomes mechanical. Learning is never cumulative, it is a movement of knowing which has no beginning and no end.

Thought continues as an unbroken stream. — It is man's original nature — in its ordinary process, thought moves forward without a halt; past, present, and future thoughts continue as an unbroken stream.

Imagination. — Recognizing the need for sound plans and ideas for the attainment of my desires, I will develop my imagination by calling upon it daily for help in the formation of my plans.

Memory. — Recognizing the value of an alert mind and an alert memory, I will encourage mine to become alert by taking care to impress it clearly with all thoughts I wish to recall and by associating those thoughts with related subjects which I may call to mind frequently.

Subconscious mind. — Recognizing the influence of my subconscious mind over my power of will, I shall take care to submit to it a clear and definite picture of my Major Purpose in life and all minor purposes leading to my major purpose, and I shall keep this picture constantly before my subconscious mind by repeating it daily!

Recollection and anticipation. — Recollection and anticipation are fine qualities of consciousness which distinguish the human mind from that of the lower animals. They are useful and serve certain purposes, but when actions are directly related to the problem of life and death they must be given up so that they will not interfere with the fluidity of mentation and the lightening rapidity of action.

Knowledge. — The remembering of previously learned material.

Comprehension. — The ability to grasp the meaning of material (usage of knowledge) by interpreting material or projecting future trends in the usage of knowledge.

Application. — The ability to use learned material in new and concrete situations.

Analysis. — The ability to break down material into component parts so that its organizational structure may be understood.

Synthesis. — The ability to put parts together to form a new whole.

Evaluation. — The ability to put parts together and to judge the value of the material for a given purpose.

Thought and thusness. — True thusness is the substance of thought, and thought is the function of true thusness. There is no thought except that of the true thusness. Thusness does not move, but its motion and function are inexhaustible.

Concepts (Abstracting)

Concepts vs. understanding. — If you learn *concepts*, if you work for information, then you don't *understand.* You only *explain.* When a man is thinking he stands off from what he is trying to understand.

Liberate yourself from concepts and see the truth with your own eyes. — It exists HERE and NOW; it requires only one thing to see it: openness, freedom — the freedom to be open and not tethered by any ideas, concepts, etc. We can go on rehearsing, analyzing, attending lectures, etc., until we are blue in the face; all this will [not] be [of] the slightest avail — it is only when we stop thinking and let go that we can start seeing, discovering. When our mind is tranquil, there will be an occasional pause to its feverish activities, there will be a let-go, and it is only then in the interval between two thoughts that a flash of UNDERSTANDING — understanding, which is not thought — can take place.

Balance your thoughts with action. — If you spend too much time thinking about a thing, you'll never get it done.

Abstract thought blinds you to life. — If you're busy with your mental computer, your energy goes into your thinking, and you don't see and hear anymore. Instead of looking directly into the fact, [one] cling[s] to forms (theories) and go[es] on entangling oneself further and further, finally putting oneself into an inextricable snare.

Concepts vs. self-actualization. — Instead of dedicating your life to actualize a concept of what you should be like, ACTUALIZE YOURSELF. The process of maturing does not mean to become a captive of conceptualization. It is to come to the realization of what lies in our innermost selves.

Life is better lived than conceptualized. — This writing can be made less demanding should I allow myself to indulge in the usual manipulating game of role creation. Fortunately for me, my self-knowledge has transcended that and I've come to understand that life is best to be lived — not to be conceptualized. If you have to *think*, you still do not *understand*.

Don't be carried away in thought. — Absence of thought is the doctrine, and it means not to be carried away by thought in the process of thought — not to be defiled by external objects — to be in thought yet devoid of thought.

Concepts prevent feeling. Don't think — FEEL. Feeling exists here and now when not interrupted and dissected by ideas or concepts. The moment we stop analyzing and let go, we can start really seeing, feeling — as one whole. There is no actor or the one being acted upon but the action itself. I stayed with my feeling then — and I felt it to the full without naming it that. At last the I and the feeling merged to become one. The I no longer feels the self to be separated from the you, and the whole idea of taking advantage of getting something out of something becomes absurd. To me, I have no other self (not to mention thought) than the oneness of things of which I was aware at that moment.

Abstract analysis is not the answer. — There is too much tendency to look inward at one's own moods, and to try and evaluate them. To stand on the outside and try to look inside is futile; whatever was there will go away. This also applies to a nebulous thing described as "Happiness." To try to identify it is like turning on a light to look at darkness. Analyze it, and it is gone.

Knowledge

Attempting to define knowledge. — The object of knowing is constantly changing. Feeling, tasting, sensational experiment, etc., are dogmas and not true knowledge as they can be wrong. Objects of perception, therefore, are ruled out of true knowledge.

Knowledge is not simply perception. — Objects of thought, rather than objects of perception, are real, more perfect, intellectual, and constant.

Knowledge vs. character. — Knowledge will give you power, but character respect.

On learning. — Learning is discovery, the discovery of the cause of our ignorance. However, the best way of learning is not the computation of information. Learning is discovering, uncovering what is there in us. When we discover, we are uncovering our own ability, our own eyes, in order to find our potential, to see what is going on, to discover how we can enlarge our lives, to find means at our disposal that will let us cope with a difficult situation. And all this, I maintain, is taking place in the here and now.

Ideas

The value of ideas. — Ideas are the beginning of all achievement — in every industry, in every profession.

Ideas are what have defined America. — Ideas are what America is looking for. Ideas have made America what she is, and one good idea will make a man what he wants to be.

New ideas are always rewarded. — It is a fact that labor and thrift produce a competence, but fortune, in the sense of wealth, is the reward of the man who can think of something that hasn't been thought of before.

Simple ideas and simple impressions. Simple ideas are copies of simple impressions. For example, I see something exciting and that certain something moves me and because of this impression I can later on have an idea of it. Therefore simple ideas are direct copies of simple impressions and cannot be broken into parts, but are a unifying whole.

Complex impressions and complex ideas. — Although complex impressions and complex ideas are in general a copy of the other (complex ideas are copies of complex impressions), in some unusual cases, they are not so. For instance, I can imagine a place where I have never been, or in the case of a man who is color blind of the color blue may make up his idea of that color with his experience of the other colors.

Three types of ideas. — Innate ideas (inborn), adventitious ideas (from outside events), factitious ideas (which one invents).

Four idea principles. — The four idea principles are:

· Find a human need, an unsolved problem

· Master all of the essentials of the problem

· Give a new "twist" to an old principle

· Believe in your idea — and act!

A five-step process to formulating ideas.

- Gather materials.

- Masticate the facts.

- Relax and drop the whole subject.

- Be ready to recognize and welcome the idea when it comes.

- Shape and develop your idea into usefulness.

On developing the creative attitude. — To develop the creative attitude, analyze, focus on the wanted SOLUTION; seek out and fill your mind with the FACTS; write down IDEAS, both sensible and seemingly wild; let the facts and ideas SIMMER in your mind; evaluate, recheck, settle on the CREATIVE IDEAS.

An idea emotionalized becomes physical. — Any idea that is constantly held in the mind and emotionalized, begins at once to clothe itself in the most convenient and appropriate physical form that is available.

An idea, by itself, is not erroneous. — The thing in which error arrives is judgment. An idea, by itself, is not erroneous but judgment makes it.

Perception

Perception is the way of truth. — Not conviction, not method, but perception is the way of truth. It is a state of effortless awareness, pliable awareness, choiceless awareness.

Perception is continuous awareness. — Require not just a moment of perception, but a continuous awareness, a continuous state of inquiry in which there is no conclusion.

A wonderful mental exercise. — When you are awake, you must be fully awake and conscious about everything. This is a wonderful mental exercise.

The perceiving mind understands truth. — There is no condemnation, no demand for a pattern of action in understanding. You are merely observing — just look at it and watch it. The perceiving mind is living, moving, full of energy, and only such a mind can understand what truth is. To see a thing uncolored by one's own personal preferences and desires is to see it in its own pristine Simplicity.

Perception implies existence to be perceived. — There is always something existing — the genuine object of our perception. Sense data is caused by physical objects, and yet sense data is not in complete resemblance with the physical object. Experience, in fact, can be said to be a constant affecting by physical objects.

The relation of sense data to the object being perceived. — Sense data is part of the surface of physical object — one is a function of the other. You can't discard either one of them. What we experience are the effects of physical objects.

The philosophical problem of perception. — What must the world be like in order for us to perceive? What do we perceive?

Notes on sense data and perception. — Sense data is caused by physical objects. In order to find out about the actual objects in front of us, reason and rational thinking are necessary. The statement "I see a T" means there *is* (existent object I see) a *T* (an inference based upon identity of the object). There are physical objects

The three layers of awareness. — Awareness covers three layers: awareness of self, the awareness of in-between (zone of fantasy), and awareness of the world.

Fear vs. awareness. — The enemy of development is this pain phobia — the unwillingness to do a tiny bit of suffering. As you feel unpleasant you interrupt the continuum of awareness and you become phobic — so therapeutically speaking we continue to grow by means of integrating awareness/attention.

Choiceless awareness is total comprehension. — Choiceless awareness: non-duality and reconciliation = TOTAL understanding. The choiceless awareness of a single and undivided mind.

In the watching lies the wonder. — Just watch choicelessly and in the watching lies the wonder. It is not an ideal, an end to be desired. The watching is a state of "being" already, not a state of "becoming."

To be a calm beholder. — Be a calm beholder of what is happening around you.

Perception is awareness without choice. — There is an awareness without choice, without any demand, an awareness in which there is no anxiety; and in that state of mind there is perception. It is the perception alone that will resolve all our problems.

Choiceless awareness is nonjudgmental observation. — Choiceless awareness — do not condemn, do not justify. Awareness works only if it's allowed free play without interference.

Do not start from a conclusion. — To understand, surely, there must be a state of choiceless awareness in which there is no sense of comparison or condemnation, no waiting for a further development of the thing we are talking about in order to agree or disagree — don't start from a conclusion above all.

"Pure seeing." — To see where there is no something (object) this is true seeing — the seeing is the result of having nothing to stand on. It is simply "pure seeing," beyond subject and object, and therefore "no-seeing."

The Ego (Self-Consciousness)

Lose the attitude. — Do not have an attitude, open yourself and focus yourself and express yourself. Reject external form that fails to express internal reality.

The ego as obstacle to acceptance. — It is the ego that stands rigidly against things coming from the outside, and it is this "ego rigidity" that makes it impossible for us to accept everything that confronts us.

On being talented. — Oftentimes people come up to me and ask, "Bruce, are you *really* that good?" I say, "Well, if I tell you I'm good, probably you will say I'm boasting; but if I tell you I'm no good, you'll know I'm lying." I have the absolute confidence not to be number two, but then I have enough sense also to realize that there can be no number one.

On social functions. — I don't like to wear stuffy clothes and be at places where everyone is trying to impress each other.

The lesson of the ego. — The point to be made about ego is that man should use his ego and not be used by ego or blinded by it.

The ego and self-suggestion. — The ego is fixed entirely by the application of self-suggestion.

Use the ego as a tool. — Those who are materialistic still hold onto the ego as though it were a possession, rather than using it as a tool. Inwardly, psychologically, be a nobody.

Repose in nothing. — Establish nothing in regard to oneself. Let things be what they are, move like water, rest like a mirror, respond like an echo, pass quickly like the nonexistent, and be quiet as purity. Those who gain, lose. Do not precede others, always follow them.

On humbleness. — To be humble to superiors is duty; to equals is courtesy; to inferiors is nobleness; and to all, safety!

To be rid of ego-consciousness. — Because one's self-consciousness or ego-consciousness is too conspicuously present over the entire range of his attention — which fact interferes with a free display of whatever proficiency he has so far acquired or is going to acquire. One should get rid of this obtruding self — or ego-consciousness — and apply himself to the work to be done as if nothing particular were taking place at the moment.

Most us suffer being self-conscious. — Most us would rather suffer being self-conscious, being looked upon, than to realize our blindness and get our eyes again — the impasse is marked by a phobic attitude (avoidance).

To be unconsciously conscious is the secret of Nirvana. — To be *consciously unconscious*, or to be *unconsciously conscious* is the secret of Nirvana. The act is so direct and immediate that intellection finds no room here to insert itself and cut it to pieces.

Ego-consciousness is clinging. — This clinging and possessive ego-consciousness, seeking to affirm itself in "liberation;" craftily tires to outwit reality by rejecting the thoughts it "possesses" and emptying the mirror of the mind, which it also "possesses" — emptiness itself is regarded as a possession and an "attainment."

The ego boundary. — The ego boundary is the differentiation between the self and the otherness. If the ego boundary is a fixed thing (which it is not) then it again becomes character, or an armor, like the turtle.

Inside and outside the ego boundary. — Inside Ego Boundary there is cohesion, love, cooperation. Outside the Ego Boundary there is suspicion, strangeness, unfamiliarity.

Turn into a doll made of wood. — Turn into a doll made of wood — it has no ego, it thinks of nothing, it is not grasping or sticky — and let the body and limbs work themselves out in accordance with the discipline they have undergone.

Self-consciousness and duality. — Consciousness of self implies a duality, the objectivation of a subject which is reflected on an object distinct from itself or which it creates as such — a complete liberation from the grip of the past, from all mental habits, and all attachment to our memories.

Transcending self-consciousness. — What man has to get over is the consciousness — the consciousness of himself. It is not "I am doing this," but rather an inner realization that "this is happening through me," or "it is doing this for me." The consciousness of self is the greatest hindrance to the proper execution of all physical action.

Seeing through ourselves. — We can see through others only when we see through ourselves.

Becoming transparent. — Lack of self-awareness renders us transparent. A soul that knows itself is opaque.

Concentration

Caution in concentration. — Concentration is a form of exclusion, and where there is exclusion, there is a thinker who excludes. It is the thinker, the excluder, the one who concentrates, that creates contradiction, because then there is a center from which there can be a deviation, a distraction.

Too much concentration belittles life. — Concentration is a narrowing down of the mind — but we are concerned with the total process of living, and to concentrate exclusively on any particular aspect of life, belittles life.

Concentration requires awareness. — A concentrated mind is not an attentive mind, but a mind that is in the state of awareness can concentrate. Awareness is never exclusive, it includes everything.

Concentration leads to success. — One great cause of failure is lack of concentration.

On Reason

Reason — the light of nature. — "The Light of Nature" is sometimes translated as "Light of Reason" (intellect).

To be guided by reason. — Recognizing that both my positive and negative emotions may be dangerous if they are not controlled and guided to desirable ends, I will submit all my desires, aims, and purposes to my faculty of reason, and I will be guided by it in giving expression to these.

The domain of logic. — Logic's central problem is the distinction between correct and incorrect argument.

Logic deals with declarative sentences. — Logic deals ONLY with declarative sentences, i.e., sentences used for the purpose of making some claim or assertion about the world.

The logician. — A logician is not concerned with the process of inference, but with the propositions which constitute the initial and end points of that process, and the relationship between them.

The proposition. — Propositions are either true or false and can be either affirmed or denied.

Premises and conclusions. — The conclusion of an argument is that proposition which is affirmed on the basis of the other proposition of the argument, and these other propositions which are affirmed as providing evidence or reasons for accepting the conclusion are the premises of that argument. However, a proposition standing alone by itself is neither a premise nor a conclusion because:

- Premise — an assumption in an argument.

- Conclusion — what follows from propositions assumed in that argument.

The art of the inference. — Inference — a process in which one proposition is arrived at and affirmed on the basis of one or more other propositions, which were accepted as the starting point of the process.

The argument. — An Argument may be considered to be any group of propositions of which one is claimed to follow from the others, which are regarded as providing evidence for the truth of that one. The structure of an argument is:

- Premise

- Conclusion

The two types of argument. — There are two types of logical arguments:

- Deductive

- Inductive

The deductive argument. — In a deductive argument the truth or falsehood of its conclusion does not determine the validity or invalidity of an argument. Nor does the validity of an argument guarantee the truth of its conclusion.

The valid argument. — A valid argument is one in which all its premises are true and, hence, its conclusion is true.

The invalid argument. — An invalid argument is one that is not valid because not all of its premises are true.

The categorical proposition. — Categorical propositions offer assertions about CLASSES, affirming or denying that one class is included in another, either in whole or in part. For example, consider the syllogism: no athletes are vegetarians; all football players are athletes; therefore, no football players are vegetarians. The premises and conclusion of the argument stated above are assertions about the class of athletes, and the class of football players.

Four standard forms of categorical propositions. — The four standard forms of categorical propositions are:

- Universal Affirmative — All S are P.

- Universal Negative — No S are P.

- Particular Affirmative — Some S are P.

- Particular Negative — Some S are not P.

It is customary to regard the word "some" as meaning "at least one."

Posteriori. — Posteriori is:

- An argument from effect to cause.

- Knowledge based on experience

Priori. — Priori is:

- Argument from cause to effect.

- Knowledge independent of experience.

The analytic proposition. — An analytic proposition is a proposition which is necessarily true because its denial is self-contradictory (e.g., all barking dogs bark).

The synthetic proposition. — A synthetic proposition is a proposition which is not self-contradictory and whose denial is not self-contradictory (e.g., all dogs bark).

The universal. — A universal is:

- What is common to many different items (e.g., redness is common to all red things). The one in the many.

- A proposition about whole of subject-class (e.g., all "s" is "p").

The particular. — A particular is:

- Single, individual, as distinct from class or universal.

- A proposition about part of a subject-class (e.g., some "s" is "p").

The Socratic method. — Plato, through the character of Socrates, has a specific method of presenting his position on a given topic. His method of argument being comprised of three steps:

· Starting with certain premises

· Through a process of reasoning, leading his opponent to

· His conclusion

Dismantling the Socratic method. — The only way to dismantle the so-called "Socratic method" of argument is also a three-step process:

· If the truth of the first is challenged successfully

· And if the remaining premises that are based on the original premise follow logically

· The conclusion is false.

Emotion

Conscience is your pilot. — Recognizing that my emotions often err in their overenthusiasm , and my faculty of reason often is without the warmth of feeling that is necessary to enable me to combine justice with mercy in my judgments, I will encourage my conscience to guide me as to what is right and what is wrong, but I will never set aside the verdicts it renders, no matter what may be the cost of carrying them out.

Muscular emotions. — Every emotion expresses itself in the muscular system. Anxiety is tremendous excitement held, bottled up.

Anger should be expressed. — Any anger that is not coming out, flowing freely, will turn into sadism, power drive, stammering, and other means of torturing.

Motors of behavior. — Emotions — the most important motors of our behavior.

Emotions and the subconscious. — The subconscious mind favors thoughts inspired by emotional feelings. It also gives preference to dominating thoughts.

Emotions are both positive and negative. — Realizing that my emotions are both Positive and negative, I will form daily Habits which will encourage the development of the positive emotions and aid me in converting the negative emotions into some form of useful action.

Happiness

Happiness is the moral measure of man. — The measure of the moral worth of a man is his happiness. The better the man, the more happiness. Happiness is the synonym of well-being.

Attaining happiness. — In order to achieve happiness or the right conduct of life, one must acquire knowledge — so he can think, reason, and create. Knowledge creates desire for the beautiful. Therefore anyone that teaches must have the knowledge of his teaching.

Simple pleasures. I like light rain. It gives one such a sense of calmness and tranquillity. I enjoy walking in the rain. But most of all, I like books. I read all types of books — fiction and nonfiction.

True fortune is a wonderful spouse. — I think when a couple marry, they either go into heaven or live in hell. They may live a fairy-tale-like life, or they may suffer a lot. I am a fortunate man. I am fortunate not because my films have broken box-office records in various parts of the world, but because I have a good wife, Linda. She is unsurpassed. Why do I say this? First, I believe a couple should develop a kind of friendship. Linda and I have this kind of friendship. We understand each other, like a pair of good friends. We thus can spend our time together happily. My wife is the luckiest thing that ever happened to me — not *The Big Boss.*

Happiness requires action. — Everybody is capable of obtaining happiness, but the matter of going on, or taking action to obtain it, is in question.

Fear

Understanding fear. — To understand your fear is the beginning of really seeing.

Intelligence and fear. — There is intelligence when you are not afraid.

Sensitivity and fear. — Sensitivity is not possible if you are afraid of this, that, etc.

Initiative and fear. — There can be no initiative if one has fear, and fear compels us to cling to tradition, gurus, etc.

Intelligence vs. authority. — The inner authority game — authority destroys intelligence.

Shame is fear of humiliation. — Shame is fear of humiliation at one's inferior status in the estimation of others.

There is fear and insecurity in pride. — Pride emphasizes the importance of the superiority of one's status in the eyes of others. There is fear and insecurity in pride, for when one aims at being highly esteemed, and having achieved such status, he is automatically involved in the fear of losing one's status. Then protection of his status appears to be his most important need, and this creates anxiety.

The fear of not being esteemed by others. — The inner self is the true self. In order to realize our true self we must be willing to live without being dependent upon the opinion of others. When we are completely self-sufficient we can have no fear of not being esteemed by others.

The more we value things, the less we value our selves. — We should devote ourselves to being self-sufficient and must not depend upon the external rating by others for our happiness. So it is true that the more we value things, the less we value our self. The more we depend upon others for esteem, the less we are self-sufficient.

Will

The will to succeed. — It's the will that makes men — success takes perseverance.

The will to do. — My will to do springs from the knowledge that I CAN DO. I'm only being natural, for there is no fear or doubt inside my mind.

The supreme court of the mind. — The power of will is the supreme court over all other departments of my mind. I will exercise it daily when I need the urge to action for any purpose, and I will form habits designed to bring the power of my will into action at least once daily.

The yielding will has a reposeful ease. — The yielding will has a reposeful ease, soft as downy feathers; a quietude, a shrinking from action. An appearance of inability to do (the heart is humble, but the work is forceful). Placidly free from anxiety, one acts in harmony with nature; one moves and revolves in the line of creation.

The will to win. — The attitude "That you can win if you want to badly enough" means that the will to win is constant and no amount of punishment, no amount of effort, or no condition is too "tough" to take in order to win. Such an attitude can be developed only if winning is closely tied to the practitioner's ideals and dreams. Experience shows that an athlete who forces himself to the limit, can keep going as long as necessary. It means that ordinary effort will not tap or release the tremendous store of reserve power latent in the human body. Extraordinary effort, highly emotionalized conditions, or a true determination to win at all costs will release this extra energy. Therefore an athlete is actually as tired as he feels, and if he is determined to win he can keep on almost indefinitely in order to achieve his objective.

Morality vs. authority. — I can walk away from millions because it's not right, but I'll be damned if I'll back up an inch from a dime because it *has* to be so.

The issue of free will. — Is free will caused by our own volition or by God (this is a theological problem of the Middle Ages) or is it governed by causal law (the term "free" then becomes the grandson of "chance"). If human actions are governed by causal law, the problem then becomes that there are no actions that are voluntary.

The will can be lethal. — There is no weapon more deadly than the will.

The will and woman. — Unquestionably man has his will — but woman has her way!

The will is spiritual. — The spiritual power of man's will removes all obstacles.

The hero is the self-willed man. — What does self-willed mean? Does it not mean "having a will of one's own?" The human herd instinct demands adaptation and subordination, but for his highest honor man elects not the meek, the pusillanimous, the supine, but precisely the self-willed man, the heroes.

Self-will is not governed by external laws. — Self-will seems to be the only virtue that takes no account of man-made laws.

Having one's own will. — What does self-willed mean? Hell, isn't it knowing above all, that, indeed, one is the captain of one's soul, the master of one's life? Now what causes such realization and, consequently, brings about a change in one's behavior? TO BE REAL, TO ACCEPT RESONSIBILITY FOR ONESELF.

The aim of the self-willed man is growth. — A self-willed man has no other aim than his own growth. He values only one thing, the mysterious power in himself which bids him live and helps him to grow. His only living destiny is the silent, ungainsayable law in his own heart, which comfortable habits make it so hard to obey but which to the self-willed man is destiny and godhead.

Good Will

Take the time to help others. — I'm not one of those guys that can brush people off. Besides, I feel that if I can just take a second to make someone happy, why not do it?

Try not to offend. — I'll not willingly offend, nor be easily offended.

To mend and to endure. — What's amiss I'll stop to mend, and endure what can't be mended.

Real living. — Real living is living for others.

Watch what you say. — Diseases enter by the mouth, misfortune issues from it.

To help one's neighbor. — If every man would help his neighbor, no man would be without help.

The noble character. — Nobility of character manifests itself at loopholes when it is not provided with large doors.

True friends are rare. — True friends are like diamonds, precious and rare. False friends are like autumn leaves, found everywhere.

Let friendships develop on their own. — Let friendship creep gently to a height; if it rushes to it, it may soon run itself out of breath.

Love and respect. — Without respect, love cannot go long.

Proficiency and harmony. — Be proficient in your field as well as in harmony among fellow men.

Kindness and remembrance. — A person cannot forget someone who is good to them.

Dreams

Dreams are future realities. — Yesterday's dreams are often tomorrow's realities.

A practical dreamer. — Be a practical dreamer backed by action.

Practical dreamers never quit. — Right now I can project my thoughts into the future. I can see ahead of me. I dream (remember that practical dreamers never quit). I may now own nothing but a little place down in a basement, but once my imagination has got up a full head of steam, I can see painted on a canvas of my mind a picture of a fine, big five- or six-story Gung Fu Institute with branches all over the States. . . I am not easily discouraged, readily visualize myself as overcoming obstacles, winning out over set backs, achieving "impossible" objectives.

Fragments of dreams are fragments of our personality. — Put the different fragments of the dream together and reown these projected, fragmented parts of our personality, and reown the hidden potential that appears in the dream. The re-owning equals the understanding of [our] projections.

The way to bring back the dream. — The way to bring back the dream is to relive the dream as IF it were happening now.

Spirituality

The difficulty of spiritual cultivation. — The cultivation of the spirit is elusive and difficult, and the tendency toward it is rarely spontaneous.

The spirit is the controlling agent of existence. — The spirit is no doubt the controlling agent of our existence (as to its whereabouts we can never tell), though altogether beyond the realm of corporeality. This invisible seat controls every movement in whatever external situation it may happen to find itself. It is thus to be extremely mobile, no "stopping" in any place at any moment.

The vital realization of the spirit. — When man comes to a conscious vital realization of those great spiritual forces within himself and begins to use those forces in science, in business, and in life, his progress in the future will be unparalleled.

Spiritual power. — Recognize and use the spiritual power of the infinite. The INTANGIBLE represents the real power of the universe. It is the seed of the tangible.

On seeking the divine within. — Whether it is the godhead or not, I feel this great force, this untapped power, this dynamic something within me. This feeling defies description, and [there is] no experience with which this feeling may be compared. It is something like a strong emotion mixed with faith, but a lot stronger.

The spiritual force transcends all. — I feel I have this great creative and spiritual force within me that is greater than faith, greater than ambition, greater than confidence, greater than determination, greater than vision. It is all these combined. My brain becomes magnetized with this dominating force which I hold in my hand.

Intensity/enthusiasm is the god within. — Intensity and/or enthusiasm is this god within us — one that instinctively becomes the art of the physical "becoming" and within this transition we no longer care to know what life means. We are indeed furnishing the "what is" by simply being.

The spirit of the universe. — The integrating principle of the whole — the spirit, as it were, of the universe — instinct with contrivance, which flows with purpose.

Contemplating heaven while living on earth. — I wish neither to possess nor to be possessed. I no longer covet paradise. More important, I no longer fear hell. If you ask me what I will do in heaven, I will say this: Why should I think about something so far away when there are so many things in this life I have not finished learning about?

Four questions on the existence of God

· Can we know God exists?

· How do we know God exists?

· What do we mean God exists?

· Do we have an idea of God?

On belief in God. — To be perfectly frank, I really do not believe in God. If there is a God, he is within. You don't ask God to give you things, you depend on God for inner theme.

On organized religion. — I have no religion whatsoever. I believe that life is a process and that man is a self-made product. The spirit of the individual is determined by his dominating thought habits.

On the divisiveness of organized religion. — Religions divide people, just as styles [in martial art] divide people. If all the religions of the world were one, the world would be united in brotherhood. Some people fight with others because they believe in different religions. If, however, they only gave the matter a bit of thought, they would never fight for such a foolish cause.

The problem with organized religion. — The source of trouble in religion is to attribute to the cause with doctrines, rules, and prejudices.

Between heaven and earth. — If you ask me, what will I do in heaven? I will say this: There are many things in this life I have not finished. Why should I think about something so far away?

The spirit is strengthened in sorrow. — Happiness is good for the body, but sorrow strengthens the spirit.

Character is the form of the soul. — Character is to the soul what outward appearance is to the body. A man's genuineness and refinement should not reveal themselves directly; they should express themselves only indirectly as an effect from within.

Let the spiritual grow up through the common. — Live content with small means; seek elegance rather than luxury, and refinement rather than fashion. Be worthy, not respectable, wealthy, not rich; study hard, think quietly, talk gently, act frankly; bear all cheerfully, do all bravely, await occasions, hurry never. In a word, let the *spiritual*, unbidden and unconscious, grow up through the common.

Let the spirit out. — Discard all thoughts of reward, all hopes of praise and fears of blame, all awareness of one's bodily self. And, finally closing the avenues of sense perception, let the spirit out, as it will.

The spirit controls the body. — The active is controlled by the inactive — the active being form or matter, and the inactive being spirit or mind.

Minimize inwardly. — It is not difficult to trim and hack off the unessential in outward physical structure. However, to shun away, to minimize inwardly is another matter.

The spirit is formless. — According to Zen, the spirit is by nature formless and no "objects" are to be harbored in it. When anything is harbored there, psychic energy loses its balance, its native activity becomes cramped, and it no longer flows with the stream. Where the energy is tipped, there is too much of it in one direction and a shortage of it in another direction. Where there is too much energy, it overflows and cannot be controlled. In either case, it is unable to cope with ever changing situations. But when there prevails a state of *purposelessness* (which is also a state of fluidity or mindlessness), the spirit harbors nothing in it, nor is it tipped in one direction; it transcends both subject and object; it responds empty-mindedly to whatever is happening.

The end of spiritual training. — Not to localize or partialize is the end of spiritual training. When it is nowhere it is everywhere. When it occupies one tenth, it is absent in the other nine-tenths. Let a person discipline himself to have the mind go on its own way, instead of trying deliberately to confine it somewhere. It is the ONE without opposite, infinite and unceasing.

PART THREE

On Matters
of Existence

Health

To flow like water. — The method for health promotion is based on water, as flowing water never grows stale. The idea is not to overdevelop or to overexert, but to normalize the function of the body.

On the joy of exercise. — I really dig exercise. When I'm jogging early in the morning, boy! It's sure refreshing. Although Hong Kong is one of the most crowded places in the world, I'm surprised how peaceful it can be in the morning. Sure, there are people, but I become oblivious to them while I am running.

On the therapeutic benefits of jogging. — Jogging is not only a form of exercise to me, it is also a form of relaxation. It is my own hour every morning when I can be alone with my thoughts.

On diet. — Only eat what your body requires, and don't [become] carried away with foods that don't benefit you.

On smoking, drinking and gambling. — I don't drink nor smoke and those events are many times senseless. I'm not a smoker because I don't think putting smoke into your body is quite the thing to do. As for alcohol, I think it tastes awful. Don't know why anyone should want to drink the stuff. As for gambling, I don't believe in getting something for nothing.

Health is a state of balance. — Health is an appropriate balance of the coordination of *all* of *what we are* (are is *being* mind rather than *having* mind). A healthy person has both a good orientation (sensoric system) and ability to act (motoric system). So if there is no balance between sensing and doing, then you are out of gear.

Courtship

Courtship is not always the proper prelude to matrimony. — Courtship is not always the proper prelude to marriage. During courtship, two people who are attracted to each other seek exciting things to do. They go dancing, they dine at fine restaurants, go to museums. They get to know all the diversions in their particular geographic locality, but they do not get to know one another.

Many successful marriages are made in college. — Many successful American marriages are made in college. There, each has a task and each can evaluate the will and the zeal with which the other approaches responsibility. In a college situation which demands application of intention, but flexibility of approach, one can learn much about one's fellow student's success with learning techniques.

Love

Honesty and love. — Frankness and truthfulness to myself and to the one I love. Truthful between two as one. You are part of my life, no pride, vanity, or anger involved.

Love is never lost. — Love is never lost. If not reciprocated it will flow back and soften and purify the heart.

Be certain of love. — I'm not one of those who do not believe in love at first sight, but I believe in taking a second look.

Absence in love. — Absence in love is like water upon fire; a little quickens, but much extinguishes it.

Love and ego. — Love is an egotism of two.

The question. — I'm loved?

Loving well and loving wisely. — I did love like a madman, but have enough sense to not love as a fool. It isn't so easy to love too well and so difficult to love wisely.

Young love vs. mature love. — Young love is a flame: very pretty, often very hot and fierce, but still only light and flickering. The love of the older and disciplined heart is as coals, deep-burning and unquenchable.

Love is mathematically just. — Love, and you shall be loved — all love is mathematically just, as much as the two sides of an algebraic equation.

Marriage

Marriage is a friendship. — Marriage is a friendship, a partnership based solidly upon ordinary, everyday occurrences.

Marriage is caring for children. — Marriage is caring for children, watching over them in sickness, training them in the way they must go, sharing worry about them and pride in them.

Marriage is everyday life. — Marriage is breakfast in the morning, work during the day — the husband at his work, the wife at hers — dinner at night, and quiet evenings together talking, reading, or watching television.

Marriage derived from everyday life lasts longer. — The happiness we have today is built on the ordinary life we had before we married. The happiness that is derived from ordinary life lasts longer; like coal, it burns gradually and slowly. The happiness that is derived from excitement is like a brilliant fire — soon it will go out. Many young couples live a very exciting life when they are in love. So, when they marry, and their lives are reduced to calmness and dullness, they will feel impatient and will drink the bitter cup of a sad marriage.

In marriage: $1/2 + 1/2 = 1$. — [My wife] and I aren't *one* and *one*. We are two *halves* that make a *whole*. You have to apply yourself to be a family — two halves fitted together are more efficient than either half would ever be alone!

Love without conditions. — The quality in Linda that moves me is her unconditional love for me. She treats our relationship with calmness[and] objectivity, and without conditions. I think this is the kind of attitude that a couple should adopt. For example, if I state a point, my wife will express her ideas on it. Certainly we ought to discuss things or it would be difficult for us to get along well.

The importance of acknowledging your love. -- A very important person I like to thank. A quality human being in her own right — giving, loving, stalwart, understanding this animal, Bruce Lee. And letting him simply be. My companion in our separate but intertwined pathways of growth, a definite enricher of my life, the woman I love; and — fortunately for me — my wife. I cannot leave this paragraph without saying that Linda, thanks for the day when, at the University of Washington, Bruce Lee had the honor to meet you.

On Raising Children

The highest standards of conduct. — Through all [my children's] education will run the Confucianist philosophy that the highest standards of conduct consist of treating others as you wish to be treated, plus loyalty, intelligence, and the fullest development of the individual in the five chief relationships of life: government and those who are governed, father and son, elder and younger brother, husband and wife, friend and friend. Equipped in that way, I don't think [they] can go far wrong.

Never strike a child. — My father never struck me — though my mother sometimes spanked me good! — and I'm not planning to strike [my children]. I think a father can control the situation by swinging with it.

Disciplining children. — I will play with my [children] and joke with my [children], but business is business. When the subject is a serious one, you don't go around trying to keep from hurting [their] feelings. You say what must be said and set the rules which must be set without worrying about whether [they] like it or not.

You are judged by your acts. — If you make an ass out of yourself, there'll always be someone ready to ride you. Showing off is the fool's idea of glory.

Education

Education vs. creativity. — What is the point of education if you in yourself are not intelligent? If you are not creative?

The nature of education. — Education consists in cultivation of intelligence (not cunning, passing exams, etc.).

The value of self-education. — Self-education makes great men.

The aim of education. — Education: to discover but not merely to imitate. Learning techniques without inward experiencing can only lead to superficiality.

Education need not be formal. — But then, how important is school? I barely made passing grades while attending the University of Washington.

Absorption vs. accumulation in education. — It is not how much you have learned, but how much you have absorbed in what you have learned — the best techniques are the simple ones executed right.

Teaching

Teaching requires a sensitive mind with great flexibility. — Above all, a teacher does not depend on a method and drill systematic routines; instead, he studies each individual student and awakens him to explore himself, both internally and externally, and ultimately integrate himself with his being. Such teaching, which is really no teaching, requires a sensitive mind with great flexibility and is difficult to come by nowadays.

A teacher is a pointer to truth, not a giver of truth. — A teacher, a good teacher that is, functions as a pointer to truth, but not a giver of truth. He employs a minimum of form to lead his student to the formless. Furthermore, he points out the importance of being able to enter a mold without being imprisoned by it, or to follow the principles without being bound by them.

The teacher cannot be fixed in a routine. — A good teacher cannot be fixed in a routine. He must not impose his student to fit a lifeless pattern, a preformulation.

The most difficult thing to teach. — A good teacher protects his pupils from his own influence. It is easy to teach one to be skillful, but it is difficult to teach him his own attitude. Each moment during teaching requires a full alert and sensitive mind that is constantly adjusting and constantly changing.

Put my words to the test. — Remember, I am no teacher; I can merely be a signpost for a traveler who is lost. It is up to you to decide on the direction. All I can offer is an experience but never a conclusion, so even what I have said needs to be thoroughly examined by you. I might be able to help you to discover and examine your problem by awakening your awareness of their cause and effect, but I cannot teach you, for I am not a teacher, and I have no style. I don't believe in system, nor in method. And without system, without method, what's to teach?

The ideal teacher. — Not "what" to think but "how" to think. [Education] after all, it is merely the root to function from. Look for ways to raise the pupil's mind above duality, to the absolute awareness which transcends it.

The six principle steps of teaching.

- Motivation of the trainee
- Maintaining their complete attention
- Promoting mental activity (thinking) — discussion, question, lecture
- Creating a clear picture of material to be learned; outlining the material
- Developing comprehension of the significance, the implications, and the practical application of the material being presented (clear goals)
- Repetition of the five preceding steps until learning has taken place

Give recognition where due. — Give recognition where it is due. Complements definitely stimulate more effort and desire to improve. Be generous with honest praising.

Teaching is a direct relationship. — I never believe in large organizations, with their domestic and foreign branches, affiliations, etc. To reach the masses, some sort of a system is required; as a result, the members are conditioned according to that system. I believe in teaching just a few, as it requires constant alert observations on each individual in order to establish a true, direct relationship.

The spiritually deficient search for external securities. — The poorer we are inwardly, the more we try to enrich ourselves outwardly.

There is no fixed teaching. — There is no fixed teaching. All I can provide is an appropriate medicine for a particular ailment. I present a possible direction, nothing more. It is like a finger pointing away to the moon; don't concentrate on the finger or you will miss all that heavenly glory.

Sincere students are rare. — Sincere and serious learners are difficult to come by. Many of them are five minute enthusiasts, some of them come in with ill intentions, but unfortunately, most of them are second-hand artists; basically conformers.

Ethics

On right conduct. — Right conduct is governed by reason and creativity.

The "good life" is a process. — The good life is a process, not a state of being. It is a direction, not a destination. The good life constitutes a direction selected by the total organism, when there is psychological freedom to move in ANY direction.

Objective standards require knowledge. — In order to establish the objective standard of correct conduct, knowledge is to be acquired.

There are no "means to ends." — There will never be means to ends, only means. And I am means. I am what I started with, and when it is all over I will be all that is left of me. All goals, apart from the means are therefore an illusion, and becoming is a denial of being.

Enrich your understanding. — Don't be in a hurry to "fix" things; rather, enrich your understanding in the ever-going process of discovery and finding more the cause of your ignorance.

Happiness is the appropriate moral behavior for the appropriate situation. — Being able to find the correct conduct for a special situation is happiness — not a strict standard for every situation.

Understanding, not a snap judgment, is required. — It need not be an immediate reaction of what [you] have heard that requires an immediate evaluation or judgement, rather shouldn't it be understanding of it, the whole situation, totally suffice?

Three most difficult things. — The three things most difficult are:

· To keep a secret

· To forget an injury

· To make good use of leisure.

Moral conduct: considerations on relative and absolute applications. — To hold moral conduct as absolute might be to hold that action is described in any old way. It might be to hold that action described in a certain way is applicable to all at all times. To hold it as relative, might be to hold it as the various function of time, geographic climate, social and economical needs, religious beliefs, etc. To hold it as relative might be to hold that the expression of right conduct might mean right conduct is the dictate of public interest, etc. To hold it as absolute might be to hold that expressing right conduct can be defined invariably.

Concerning objective and subjective value judgments. — A judgment is objective if it concerns objective questions; a subjective judgment is one which concerns one's personal view on the objective. Objective is factual. Subjective is a matter of opinion. There is a big difference between why you THINK something is wrong and to justify, explaining, proving that something is wrong. A concept is objective if the quality denoted is the actual quality of action (inherent in the objective).

The two primary moral questions. — There are two sorts of problems concerning moral issues:

· Where does good or bad action derive from?

· What makes an action bad or good?

The trouble of man. — Honor and disgrace are alike a cause of excitement. The trouble of man lies in the love for self.

Poverty and peace. — Any poor country or person is hostile while they are down. If you have nothing, you can afford to be hostile. But wait until they, too, become more prosperous. They will soon quiet down and want peace just like the rest of the world.

Humility leads to honor. — Humility forms the basis of honor, just as the low ground forms the foundation of a high elevation.

The four ethical theories. — There are four different ethical theories:

- Objective Theory of Ethics — that goodness is objective (Plato's theory) and cannot be further deduced.

- Consequential Theory of Ethics — that what makes an action good is its outcome (utilitarianism for instance); the most pleasure for the most people (more believable than objectivism as mentioned).

- Motivational Theory of Ethics — that moral character of an action springs from a motive of the actor — it is not a bad action so long as a person has good intentions (Immanuel Kant is one of the motivational theorists; he said "do not perform any action that you cannot rationalize for people to act all the time.")

- Approbative Theory of Ethics — to say that an action is good or bad depends on the approval of others.

The intrinsic value of the good and beautiful. — To value them all by themselves. Not to value them in their manifestation.

On my character. — To be honest and all that, I'm not as bad as some of them, but I definitely am not saying that I am a *saint!*

Racism

On the Brotherhood of Man. — If I say that "everyone under the sun is a member of a universal family," you may think that I am bluffing and idealistic. But if anyone still believes in racial differences, I think he is too backward and narrow. Perhaps he still does not understand man's equality and love.

Under the heavens there is but one family. — Basically, human traits are the same everywhere. I don't want this to sound like "As Confucius say," but under the sky, under the heavens, there is but one family.

Tradition is the root of racism. — Many people are still bound by tradition; when the elder generation says "no" to something, then these other people will strongly disap prove of it as well. If the elders say that something is wrong, then they also will believe that it is wrong. They seldom use their mind to find out the truth and seldom express sincerely their real feeling. The simple truth is that these opinions on such things as racism are *traditions*, which are nothing more than a "formula" laid down by these elder people's experience. As we progress and time changes, it is necessary to reform this formula.

Being free of tradition, one holds no prejudice. — I, Bruce Lee, am a man who never follows these formulas of the fear-mongers. So, no matter if your color is black or white, red or blue, I can still make friends with you without any barrier.

Adversity

Adversity is beneficial to us. — Prosperity is apt to prevent us from examining our conduct; but adversity leads us to think properly of our state, and so is beneficial to us.

Adversity causes the mind to think properly. — In a time when everything goes well, my mind is pampered with enjoyment, possessiveness, etc. Only in times of adversity, privation, or mishap, does my mind function and think properly of my state. This close examination of self strengthens my mind and leads me to understand and be understood.

The value of foolish questions. — A wise man can learn more from a foolish question than a fool can learn from a wise answer.

Never waste energy on worries and negative thoughts. — I mean who has the most insecure job as I have? What do I live on? My faith in my ability that I'll make it. Sure my back screwed me up good for a year but with every adversity comes a blessing because a shock acts as a reminder to oneself that we must not get stale in routine.

Anxiety is a defense. — Don't be forecasting evil unless it is what you can guard against. Anxiety is good for nothing if we can't turn it into a defense.

There is no shame in losing. — It is not a shame to be knocked down by other people. The important thing is to ask when you're being knocked down, "Why am I being knocked down?" If a person can reflect in this way, then there is hope for this person.

To be able to do the things we want sometimes requires the performance of a few we don't. — Just as the maintaining of good health may require the taking of unpleasant medicine, so the condition of being able to do the things we enjoy often requires the performance of a few we don't. Remember my friend that it is not what happens that counts, it is how you react to them. Your mental attitude determines what you make of it, either a stepping stone or stumbling block.

Sorrow as educator. — Sorrows are our best educator. A man can see further through a tear than a telescope.

The forms of stupidity. — Stupidity assumes two forms, it speaks or is silent. Mute stupidity is bearable.

The world is full of troublemakers. — The world is full of people who are determined to be somebody or give trouble. They want to get ahead to stand out. Such ambition has no use for a man of Tao, who rejects all forms of self-assertiveness and competition

Adversity shocks you to higher levels. — With adversity you are shocked to higher levels, much like a rain storm that is so violent, but yet afterwards all plant grows.

Adversity is like a rainfall. — Adversity is like the period of the former and of the latter rain: cold, comfortless, unfriendly to man and to animal; yet from that season have their birth the flower and the fruit, the date, the rose, and the pomegranate.

Defeat is education. — What is defeat? Nothing but education; nothing but the first step to something better.

In solitude you are least alone. — Loneliness is only an opportunity to cut adrift and find yourself. In solitude you are least alone. Make good use of it.

The value of frustration. — Without frustration you will not discover that you might be able to do something on your own. We grow through conflict.

Bear insults patiently. — There is nothing that will enable you to pursue your course in greater peace than the patient bearing of insult. Patience is not passive, on the contrary it is concentrated strength.

Be cautious whom you trust. — Don't easily trust anyone on this earth because there are all kinds.

The wise can draw advantage from mishap. — No accidents are so unlucky but that the wise may draw some advantage from them; nor are there any so lucky but that the foolish may turn them to their own prejudice.

Anxiety. — *Anxiety* is the gap between the *NOW* and the *THEN*. So if you are in the *NOW*, you can't be anxious, because your excitement flows immediately into ongoing spontaneous activity.

The critic. — Empty heads have long tongues. Commonly they, whose tongue is their weapon, use their feet for defense.

There are always obstacles on the road to achievement. — Believe me that in every big thing or achievement there are always obstacles, big or small, and the reaction one shows to such obstacles is what counts, not the obstacle itself. There is no such thing as defeat until you admit so yourself, but not until then!

Inner resistance is not the solution. — Whether I like it or not, circumstances are thrust upon me, and being a fighter at heart I sort of fight it in the beginning but soon realize what I need is not inner resistance and needless conflict (in the form of dissipation); rather, by joining forces to readjust and make the best of it.

Don't add worry to your troubles. — Serene, detached from all results, ready to fight or run, to win or lose, and always ready to laugh at all things, take whatever comes. Your child is ill you say, or you cannot pay the rent? Very well, accept these facts and face them. Are they not trouble enough in themselves without adding the aggravation of worry to them?

You cannot clear muddied water with your hand. — Who is there that can make muddy water clear? But if allowed to remain still, it will become clear of itself. Who is there that can secure a state of absolute repose? But keep calm and let time go on, and the state of repose will gradually arrest.

Worry only creates problems for those around you. — One who is possessed by worry not only lacks the poise to solve his own problems, but by his nervousness and irritability creates additional problems for those around him.

Learn to walk on. — Why add the tension of emotion/ thought to a situation which is illusion, to the extent that it is real, of a passing moment (in any event, the result of previous causes)? Do what seems wise to be done, forget it, and walk on. Walk on and see a new view. Walk on and see the birds fly. Walk on and leave behind all things that would dam up the inlet, or clog the outlet, of experience.

Confrontation

Avoid trials of skill. — Avoid trials of skill; at first it's all friendliness but in the end it's all antagonism.

Avoid distraction and rivalry. — Shut out all forms of distraction. Eliminate all opportunities for rivalry.

On people who "challenge." — These people must have something wrong in their hearts. For if their heart was right, they would not challenge other people to fight. Moreover, most of these people challenge because they feel insecure and want to use a fight as a means to achieve some unknown aim.

Do not anticipate the outcome. — The great mistake is to anticipate the outcome of the engagement; you ought not to be thinking of whether it ends in victory or in defeat.

On being challenged. — I have learned that being challenged means one thing and that is what is *your* reaction to it? How does it affect *you*? Now if you are secure within yourself, you treat it very, very lightly. Because you ask yourself: *Am I really afraid of that man?* Or *Do I have any doubt within me that he is going to get me?* And if I do not have such doubt, and if I do not have such fear, I would certainly treat it very lightly — just as today the rain is going on strong, but tomorrow, baby, the sun is going to come out again.

All disputes can be settled by law. — Nowadays you don't go around on the street kicking people or punching people, because if you do [someone will simply pull out a gun and] — bang! That's it. I don't care how good you are in martial art. Today everything can be settled by law. Even if you want to avenge your father, you need not challenge one to a fight.

You control the confrontation. — No one can hurt you unless you allow him to.

See through the illusion. — See that there is no one to fight, only an illusion to see through. Be aware of illusions!

The need for transcendence. — A struggle of any nature can never be settled satisfactorily until the absolute fact is touched. Where neither opponent can affect the other. Not neutrality, not indifference, but TRANSCENDENCE is the thing needed.

Adaptability

On the nature of adaptation. — What is adaptation? It is like the immediacy of the shadow adjusting itself to the moving body.

The importance of adaptation. — The inability to adapt brings destruction.

Adaptation is stillness in movement. — The stillness in stillness is not the real stillness; only when there is stillness in movement does the universal rhythm manifest.

Adaptation is wisdom. — Wisdom does not consist in trying to wrest the good from the evil but in learning to "ride" them as a cork adapts itself to the crests and troughs of the waves.

The adaptive mind. — That of not being tense but ready, not thinking but not dreaming, not being rigidly set but flexible. Aware and alert, ready for whatever may come.

Be flexible to change with change. — Be flexible so you can change with change. Empty yourself! Open up! After all, the usefulness of a cup is in its emptiness.

Change is changeless. — To change with change is the changeless state.

Stillness in movement. — The stillness in stillness is not the real stillness, only when there is stillness in movement does the universal rhythm manifest.

On interchangeability. — The flow of movements is in their interchangeability.

Adaptability is intelligence. — Intelligence is sometimes defined as the capacity of the individual to adjust himself successfully to his environment, or to adjust the environment to his needs.

Bend and survive. — There is another bit of Chinese philosophy that has a bearing on problems common to all human kind. We say, "The oak tree is mighty, yet it will be destroyed by a mighty wind because it resists the elements; the bamboo bends with the wind, and by bending, survives."

The Parable of the Butcher. — There was a fine butcher who used the same knife year after year, yet it never lost its delicate, precise edge. After a lifetime of service, it was still as useful and effective as when it was new. When asked how he had preserved his knife's fine edge, he said. "I follow the line of the hard bone. I do not attempt to cut it, nor to smash it, nor to contend with it in any way. That would only destroy my knife." In daily living, one must follow the course of the barrier. To try to assail it will only destroy the instrument. And no matter what some people will say, barriers are not the experience of any one person, or any one group of persons. They are the universal experience.

Adapt like water. — Be like water; water has form and yet it has no form. It is the softest element on earth, yet it penetrates the hardest rock. It has no shape of its own, yet it can take any shape in which it is placed. In a cup, it becomes the shape of the cup. In a vase, it takes the shape of the vase and curls about the stems of flowers. Put it in a teapot, it becomes the teapot. Please observe the adaptability of water. If you squeeze it fast, the water will flow out quickly. If you squeeze it slowly, it will come out slowly. Water may seem to move in contradiction, even uphill, but it chooses any way open to it so that it may reach the sea. It may flow swiftly or it may flow slowly, but its purpose is inexorable, its destiny sure.

Philosophy

Study philosophy. — Read all kinds of the books of man — the central themes, the styles, the advantages, the disadvantages.

The importance of reading. — Reading, specialized reading, is the mental food.

On philosophy. — Philosophy has been defined throughout the years as the "Love of Wisdom." Its purpose is to investigate things through a process of logical thinking and reasoning. Philosophy has no interest in "how," rather it is concerned with "what" and "why."

The pleasures of philosophy. — When I enrolled in the University of Washington and was enlightened by philosophy, I regretted all my previous immature assumptions. My majoring in philosophy was closely related to the pugnacity of my childhood. I often ask myself these questions:

· What comes after victory?

· Why do people value victory so much?

· What is "glory"?

· What kind of "victory" is "glorious"?

Philosophy reveals what man lives for. — When my tutor assisted me in choosing my courses, he advised me to take up philosophy because of my inquisitiveness. He said, "philosophy will tell you what man lives for."

On the process of Western philosophy. — The process of philosophy is to get or obtain clear information on virtually any topic, but certain philosophers, such as Plato, have as their focal point the realm of ethics and morality. Specifically, issues that deal with "good" and "bad," what constitutes the "ideal life" that one ought to strive for.

Philosophy is in danger of becoming something that is simply professed. — Many philosophers are among those who say one thing and do another, and the philosophy that a man professes is often quite other than the one he lives by. Philosophy, therefore, is in danger of becoming more and more only something professed.

Living vs. theorizing. — Philosophy is not "living" but an activity concerning theoretic knowledge, and most philosophers are not going to live things, but simply to theorize about them, to contemplate them. And to contemplate a thing implies maintaining oneself outside it, resolved to keep a distance between it and ourselves.

The disease of philosophy. — Philosophy is itself the disease for which it pretends to be the cure: the wise man does not pursue wisdom but lives his life, and therein precisely does his wisdom lie.

Philosophy often strives to convert reality into a problem. — In life, we accept naturally the full reality of what we see and feel in general with no shadow of a doubt. Philosophy, however, does not accept what life believes, and strives to convert reality into a problem. Like asking such questions as: "Is this chair that I see in front of me really there?" "Can it exist by itself?" Thus, rather than making life easy for living by living in accord with life, philosophy complicates it by replacing the world's tranquillity with the restlessness of problems.

Rationalism. — Rationalism is related to Intuitionism. The rationalist holds that reason is capable of grasping basic truths intuitively and deriving other truths from them by rational procedures, logical demonstration. In less extreme forms, reason and reason's evidence are necessary to distill out of sense experience, or impart to sense experience universal necessary laws.

Empiricism. — Empiricism emphasizes the importance of experience in knowledge. Recent empiricists tend to give a larger role to reason in the organization of knowledge, stressing scientific method (with its theoretical, mathematical, conceptual structure, as well as its experimental approach) as contrasted with simple perception. They emphasize the tentative, hypothetical-experimental, and self-corrective character of science.

On Existentialism. — Existentialism wants to do away with concepts, and to work on the awareness principle, on phenomenology. The set back with the present existentialist philosophies is that they need their support from somewhere else. If you look at the existentialists, they say that they are nonconceptual, but if you look at the people, they all borrow concepts from other sources. Buber from Judaism, Tillich from Protestantism, Sartre from Socialism, Heidegger from language, Binswanger from psychoanalysis.

PART FOUR

On
Achievement

Work

The practical nature of the world. — This world is very practical. You do more work, you get rewarded more; you do less work, you lose your rewards.

Something for something. — There is only something for something, never something for nothing.

More work equals more rewards. — It's the law of averages: put in more, come out with more.

The reward is to be found in the work. — The important thing is that I am personally satisfied with my work. If it is a piece of junk, I will only regret it.

It's not the job, but how you do it. — It's not what you give, it's the way you give it.

The reward should be proportionate to the work. — No one ever does anything with enthusiasm unless he benefits thereby — reward proportionately.

Intense desire creates its own talents and opportunities. — We are told that talent creates its own opportunities. But it sometimes seems that intense desire creates not only its own opportunities, but its own talents.

Two ways of making a good living. — There are two ways of making a good living. One is the result of hard working, and the other, the result of the imagination (requires work, too, of course). Some may not believe it, but I spent hours perfecting whatever I did.

One's moral virtue is reflected in one's work. — The moral worth of a man influences what his job should be. Once he functions the way he ought to, he is happy.

Attaining happiness in work. — In order that people may be happy in their work these three things are needed:

- They must be for it.
- They must not do too much of it.
- They must have a sense of success in it.

Never prostitute your principles in your work. — I will never prostitute myself in any way that I do what I don't believe in.

On the need to hold something in reserve. — Don't enter into anything with a totality of spirit. Something must be held back. The Occidental homily is *"Don't put all your eggs in one basket,"* but it is spoken of material things. I refer to the emotional, intellectual, spiritual. I can illustrate my beliefs by what I practice in my own life. I have a lot to learn as an actor. I am learning. I am investing much of myself in it, but not all.

On office work. — I never wanted a job in an office or any job that I had to work eight hours a day at — day in and day out. I don't think I could have stood it. I'm not the type of guy who can sit in the office doing the same routine day in and day out. I have to do something that is creative and interesting to me.

Quality

On perfection. — I don't want to do anything half way; it has to be perfect.

A sincere desire to do it right. — I couldn't go wrong because what I always like about myself is this stickability toward quality and the sincere desire to do it right.

The reward is in the action, not from it. — My only sure reward is "in" my actions and not "from" them. The quality of my reward is in the depth of my response, the centralness of the part of me I act from.

Quality means a lot. — Ever since I was a kid, the word "quality" has meant a lot to me. Somehow I know and am devoting sincerely myself to it with much sacrifice and heading toward a direction; you can rest assured that Mr. Quality himself will always be there.

Do more than your duty. — If you want to do your duty properly, you should do just a little more than that.

Aim at perfection in all endeavors. — Aim at perfection in everything, though in most things it is unattainable; however, they who aim at it, and persevere, will come much nearer to it than those whose laziness and despondency make them give it up as unattainable.

If you must be a product, be the best product. — Oftentimes businesspeoplesee not a human being but a product, a commodity. However, you, as a human being, have the right to be the best goddamn product that ever walked and work so hard that the businesspeople have to listen to you. You have that personal obligation to yourself to make yourself the best *product* possible according to your own terms. Not the *biggest* or the *most successful*, but the *best quality* — with that achieved, comes everything else.

Quality is the highest value. — What I honestly value more than anything else is *quality*: doing one's best in the manner of the responsibility and craftsmanship of a Number One.

Motivation

Your mind determines the effect. — Everyone — no matter who he is or where — must know from childhood that whatever occurs, does not happen if the occurrence isn't allowed to come into the mind. It is not what happens in our life that is important, it's how we react to what happens. Failure is what your mind acknowledges.

Suffering is mostly self-manufactured. — Joy and suffering are the fruit of right and wrong thinking. Suffering, especially, is mostly self-manufactured; we are never so happy or so unhappy as we suppose. To go one step beyond, according to Taosim, suffering and joy are one!

Defeat is a state of mind. — Defeat is a state of mind; no one is ever defeated until defeat has been accepted as a reality.

Defeat is temporary. — To me, defeat in anything is merely temporary, and its punishment is but an urge for me to greater effort to achieve my goal. Defeat simply tells me that something is wrong in my doing; it is a path leading to success and truth.

Don't choose to waste energy. — Never waste energy on worries or negative thoughts. All problems are brought into existence — drop them.

To be discouraged is to be defeated. — It is not what happens that is success or failure, but what it does to the heart of man. No man is defeated unless he is discouraged.

The problem is in anticipation of suffering. — Suffering itself does less afflict the senses than the anticipation of suffering.

Become what you think. — What you HABITUALLY THINK largely determines what you will ultimately become.

Know the difference between a catastrophe and an inconvenience. — To realize that it's just an inconvenience, that it is not a catastrophe, but just an unpleasantness, is part of coming into your own, part of waking up.

Stumbling blocks and stepping stones. — Are you going to make your obstacles stepping stones to your dreams, or stumbling blocks because unknowingly you let negativeness, worries, fear, etc., take over you?

The change is from inner to outer. — We start by dissolving our attitude not by altering outer conditions.

Refuse to stay down. — In Chinese variety stores we have a weighted dog, like your weighted clowns, which points out a moral: "Fall down nine times, but rise again ten times." To refuse to be cast down, that is the lesson.

Choose the positive. — You have your choice — you are master of your attitude — choose the POSITIVE, the CONSTRUCTIVE. Optimism is a faith that leads to success.

Cease negative mental chattering. — If you think a thing is impossible, you'll make it impossible. Pessimism blunts the tools you need to succeed.

Goals

Goals give life substance. — To strive actively to achieve some goal gives your life meaning and substance.

Three questions. — Come to some sort of realization as to whatever your pursuit might be. In my case, it has been the pursuit of becoming, moment to moment. And constantly questioning myself: "What is this, Bruce?" "Is it true or not true?" "Do you really mean it or not mean it?" Once I've found that out, that's it.

A goal is not always meant to be reached. — A goal is not always meant to be reached. It often serves simply as something to aim at.

Don't fear failure. — Not failure, but low aim, is the crime. In great attempts it is glorious even to fail.

The first rule of achieving your goal. — Know what you want. I know my idea is right, and, therefore, the results would be satisfactory. I don't really worry about the reward, but to set in motion the machinery to achieve it. My contribution will be the measure of my reward and success. When you drop a pebble into a pool of water, the pebble starts a series of ripples that expand until they encompass the whole pool. This is exactly what will happen when I give my ideas a definite plan of action.

Thoughts are things. — Thoughts are things, in the sense that thought can be translated into its physical equivalent.

Mixing thought with definiteness of purpose. — I begin to appreciate now the old saying "he can because he thinks he can." I believe that anybody can think himself into his goal if he mixes thought with definiteness of purpose, persistence; and a burning desire for its translation into reality.

Daily progress. — Make at least one definite move daily toward your goal.

The future can give you happiness. — The past is history and only the future can give you happiness. So, everybody must prepare for their future and create their own future.

One rarely reaches the goal in one step. — The control of our being is not unlike the combination of a safe. One turn of the knob rarely unlocks the safe. Each advance and retreat is a step toward one's goal.

Attitude determines altitude. — You will never get any more out of life than you expect. Every man today is the result of his thoughts of yesterday.

Always keep your goals in focus. — Keep your mind on the things you want and off those you don't.

Faith

Faith vs. doubt. — I respect faith, but doubt is what gets you an education.

To act on faith. — Faith without work is death.

Applied faith. — Faith backed by action is applied faith.

The power of faith. — Thoughts backed by faith will overcome all obstacles.

Faith in oneself. — What do I live on? My faith in my ability that I'll make it. Faith makes it possible to achieve that which man's mind can conceive and believe. It is a well-known fact that one comes, finally, to believe whatever one repeats to one's self, whether the statement be true or false. If a man repeats a lie over and over, he will eventually accept the lie as truth. Moreover, he'll *believe* it to be the truth. Every man is what he is because of the dominating thoughts which he permits to occupy his mind.

Faith is a state of mind. — Faith is a state of mind that can be conditioned through self-discipline. Faith will accomplish.

Cultivating faith. — Faith can be induced or created by affirmation or repeated instructions to the subconscious mind through the principle of autosuggestion. This is the only known method of voluntary development of the emotion of faith.

Faith and reason. — I cannot and will not "scoff" at faith when reason seems to be such a barren thing.

Faith maintains the soul. — Faith is the maintaining of the soul through which one's aims may be translated into their physical equivalent.

Success

Success — a definition. Success means doing something sincerely and whole-heartedly. And you have to have the help of other people to achieve it.

Success is not luck. — I don't believe in pure luck. You have to create your own luck. You have to be aware of the opportunities around you and take advantage of them.

Success is when preparation meets opportunity. — Opportunities may come your way or they may not. Luck may come your way or it may not. But if they come your way — and you call that luck — you'd better be ready for it!

On being success-conscious. — Probably, people will say I'm too conscious of success. Well, I am not. Success comes to those who become success-conscious. If you don't aim at an object, how the heck on earth do you think you can get it?

Climbing the ladder of success is a fantasy. — As for the idea of climbing higher [up the ladder of success], I think that it is very absurd; it is only a fantasy. It cannot be obtained just by sitting here and speculating. Although today I am successful, I will still continue to discover myself. But whether I can "climb higher" is still a fantasy.

The price of success. — He who wants to succeed should learn how to fight, to strive, and to suffer. You can acquire a lot in life, if you are prepared to give up a lot to get it.

The biggest disadvantage of success. — The biggest disadvantage of success is losing your privacy. It's ironic but we all strive to become wealthy and famous, but once you're there, it's not all rosy.

Success complicates simplicity. — To many, the word "success" seems to be a paradise, but now that I'm in the midst of it, it is nothing but circumstances that seem to complicate my innate feeling toward simplicity and privacy.

Success is not a destination. — Remember, success is a journey, not a destination. Have faith in your ability. You will do just fine.

The eternal condition of success. — A purpose is the eternal condition of success.

The three keys to success. — Persistence, persistence, and persistence. The Power can be created and maintained through daily practice — continuous effort.

Money

The nature of money. — Money of itself has no explicit nature. Money is what one makes of it.

Money is a means, not an end. — A child must be taught early that money is only a means, a *type* of usefulness, an implement. Like all instruments, it has certain purposes, but it will not do everything. One must learn how to use it, what it will do, but above all what it will not do.

Money is an indirect matter. — My policy is that money is an indirect matter. The direct matter is your ability or what you are going to do that counts. If that comes, the indirect things will follow.

A fair share of the profit. — Many film producers think I am only interested in money. That's why they all try to lure me on to their set by promising me huge sums and nothing else. But, at heart, I only want a fair share of the profit.

The good times will not always last. — I profited from my father's philosophy about money. He used to tell me, "If you make 10 dollars this year, always think to yourself that next year you may only make five dollars — so be prepared."

Keep money in perspective. — Sure money is important in providing for my family and giving us what we want. But it isn't everything.

Enjoying your work is the important thing. — At [one] time I wanted all the indirect things — money, fame, the big opening nights. Now I have it, or am beginning to get it, the whole thing doesn't seem important any more. I have found that *doing* a thing is more important. I am having fun doing it. Money comes second.

Fame

On the illusion of stardom. — A "star" is an illusion. Man, is that something that can screw you up. When the public calls you a star, you had better know that it's only a game. If you believe and enjoy all those flatteries (yes, we are only human and we all do, to a certain extent), and forget the fact that the same people who once were your "pals" might just desert you to make friends with another "winner" the moment you no longer are, well, it's your choice. You own your right (though it needs some self-inquiry here, it is still your choice; you have that right).

Stars rise and fall. — Stars rise and then fall. This is not surprising. Many of them do not understand themselves, so after their failure, they will feel disheartened. They should ask themselves if they had any substantial reason to support their success, or if they succeeded through luck. If they are willing to calm down and reexamine themselves, they will feel better. But it's been my experience that not many stars are like this. When they succeed, they are blind, thinking that they are the greatest star in the world. So, in the end, when the god of luck leaves them, they feel unfortunate.

The abuse of stardom. — There are too many stars and too few actors. Box-office popularity often provides the stars with considerable power. Unfortunately, many tend to misuse it.

Don't be blinded by success. — When you become successful, when you become famous, it's very, very easy to be blinded by all these happenings. Everybody comes up to you when you have long hair [and] they'll say "Hey, that's *in*, baby, *that's the in thing.*" But if you have no name, they'll say "Boy, look at that disgusting juvenile delinquent."

Flattery

The two diseases [of the ego]. — The two diseases are riding an ass to search for an ass, and riding an ass and being unwilling to dismount.

The six diseases [of excessive self-consciousness]. — The six diseases are:

- The desire for victory
- The desire to resort to technical cunning
- The desire to display all that he has learned
- The desire to overawe the enemy
- The desire to play a passive role
- The desire to get rid of whatever disease he is likely to be infected with

Beware the "yes" people. — I mean, too many people are *"yes, yes, yes"* to you all the time, you see. So, unless you really at that time understand what life is about and that, right now, man, some game is happening and realize that it is a game — fine and dandy. Then that's all right. But most people tend to be blinded by it because if things are repeated too many times, you start to believe it.

The insincerity of those asking for advice. — Nothing is less sincere than our mode of giving and asking advice. He who asks seems to have deference for the opinion of his friend, while he only aims to get approval of his own [opinion] and make his friend responsible for his action. And he who gives repays the confidence supposedly placed in him by a seemingly disinterested zeal, but he seldom means anything by his advice but his own interest or reputation. When a man seeks your advice he generally wants your praise.

PART FIVE

On Art
and Artists

Art

Art is the expression of the self. — Art is really the expression of the self. The more complicated and restricted the method, the less the opportunity for the expression of one's original sense of freedom.

Art and choiceless awareness. — Artists in all fields must learn to observe choicelessly, to digest their observations, and to express them in their work.

Art begins with feelings. — Art must originate with an experience or feeling of the artist.

Art and emotion. — Art is communication of feelings.

Forget your mind and become one with the work. — If [one] has any idea at all of displaying his art well, he ceases to be a good artist, for his mind "stops" with every movement he goes through. In all things, it is important to forget your "mind" and become one with the work at hand.

Art requires creativity and freedom. — Art lives where absolute freedom is, because where it is not, there can be no creativity — art has no ego rigidity.

Art is not decorative. — Art is never decoration, embellishment; instead it is work of enlightenment. Art, in other words, is a technique for acquiring liberty.

The aim of art. — The aim of art is to project an inner vision into the world without.

The artistic requisite. — Requirement to be an artist: purity of heart.

Art is transcendent. — Art is an expression of life and transcends both time and space.

Art is the music of the soul made visible. — Behind every motion is the music of his soul made visible. Otherwise empty motion is like an empty word; no meaning. Postures without proper channeling of your emotions behind them are dead movements.

Art demands whole-hearted action. — Art demands only immediated, honest and whole-hearted action. Through art our own souls are what we must employ to give a new form and a new meaning to Nature or the world.

Art is psychic understanding. — Art reveals itself in psychic understanding of the inner essence of things, and gives form to the relation of man with NOTHING, with the nature of the absolute. Creation in art is the psychic unfolding of the personality, which is rooted in the Nothing. Its effect is a deepening of the personal dimension of the soul.

Art is developed by soulful reflection. — Art calls for complete mastery of techniques, developed by reflection within the soul.

Artless art is the art of the soul. — "Artless art" is the artistic process within the artist and its meaning is "Art of the Soul." All the various moves of all the tools mean a step on the way to the absolute aesthetic world of the soul.

Artistic skill must radiate from the human soul. — Artistic skill, therefore, does not mean artistic perfection. It remains rather a continuing medium or reflection of some step in psychic development, the perfection of which is not to be found in shape and form, but must radiate from the human soul. The artistic activity does not consist in art itself as such; it penetrates into a deeper world in which all art forms of things inwardly experienced flow together, and in which the harmony of soul and cosmos in the nothing has its outcome in reality.

The task of art. — The task of art is so to state in aesthetic creation the deepest psychic and personal experiences of a human being [so] as to enable those experiences to be intelligible and generally recognized within the total framework of an ideal world.

Art reflects the soul. — It is the art of the soul at peace — like moonlight mirrored in a deep lake.

An artist must be an artist of life. — The ultimate aim is to use his daily activity to become a past master of life, and so as to lay hold of the art of living. Masters in all branches of art must first be masters in living, for the soul creates everything.

Art leads to the essence of life. — Art is the way to the Absolute and to the essence of human life — creative action, with sensitivity, that positive state of innocence.

Art is the perfection of nature. — Art is the perfection of nature and life through the artist, who has supreme control of technique and is thereby liberated from it.

Art opens all human capacities. — The aim of art is not the one-sided promotion of spirit, soul, and the senses, but the OPENING of all human capacities — thought, feeling, and will — to the life rhythm of the world of nature: so will the voiceless voice be heard and the self be brought into harmony with it.

Immediacy in art. — Would that we could at once paint with the eyes! In the long way from the eye through the arm to the pencil, how much is lost!

If we cling to any artistic technique it can limit our artistic expression. — Art is the expression of the self; the more complicated and restrictive a method is, the lesser the opportunity for expression of one's original sense of freedom. The techniques, although they play an important role in the earlier stage, should not be too complex, restrictive, or mechanical. If we cling to them, we will become bound by their limitations.

Seamless art is perfect art. — The perfection of art is to conceal art.

Pseudo-art is the result of insincerity. — Much pseudo-art comes from insincerity or the attempt to create a work of art which does not grow from an actual experience or feeling.

The four postulates of effective art. — Adequate form [in art] requires:

- Individuality rather than imitative repetitiousness
- Brevity rather than bulkiness
- Clarity rather than obscurity
- Simplicity of expression rather than complexity of form.

Art requires soulful commitment. — There are simply not enough soulful characters who are committed, dedicated, and at the same time professional.

True art cannot be handed out. — I insist and maintain that art — true art that is — cannot be handed out. Furthermore, art is never decoration or embellishment. Instead it is a constant process of *maturing* (in the sense of NOT having arrived!).

Art is a means of acquiring personal liberty. — Art, after all, is a means of acquiring "personal" liberty. Your way is not my way nor mine yours.

The way of the artist. — With all the training thrown to nowhere, with a mind (if there is such a verbal substance) perfectly unaware of its own working, with the "self" vanishing nowhere, art attains its perfection.

The true artist has no public. — The true artist has no public; he works for the sheer joy of it, with an element of playfulness, of casualness. Art reaches its greatest peak when devoid of self-consciousness. Freedom discovers man the moment he loses concern over what impression he is making or about to make.

The last step of art is simplicity. — Simplicity is the last step of art and the beginning of nature.

Where art abides. — Art lives where ABSOLUTE FREEDOM is, because where it is not, there can be no creativity.

On the point of art. — The point is to utilize the art as a means to advance in the study of the *Way*.

In search of a dedicated artist. — As in the combative arts, to train a deliverer and make him ready, mentally and physically, is difficult enough, and to find one with just that right appropriateness and that rare quality of a dedicated artist, can happen once in a blue moon.

Film-making

Longing to make a really good film. — What I long for is to make a really good movie. But, unfortunately, few local producers can live up to my expectations. In fact, I would be quite happy to sit down for a long talk with any one who takes filming seriously. I would be quite satisfied even if it's just talks.

Film-making is a marriage of business and art. — It is an unfortunate fact but still a cold fact that cinema is a marriage of business and art, in Hollywood or Hong Kong.

Don't glorify violence. — I don't think one should use violence and aggression as themes of movies. The glorification of violence is bad.

Starting new trends. — What I am trying to do is start a whole trend of martial art films in the U.S. To me, they are much more interesting and exciting than the gunslinging sagas of the West. In the westerns you are dealing solely with guns. Here we deal with everything. It is an expression of the human body.

The creative benefit of directing. — I want to direct more films. Directing, I feel, is more creative. You really get a chance to produce the result you want.

Acting

The quality actor. — Just what then is an actor of quality? To begin with, he is no *"movie star,"* which is nothing but an abstract word given by the people and a symbol. There are more people who want to become "movie stars" than actors. To me, an actor is the sum total of all that he is — his high level of understanding of life, his appropriate good taste, his experience of happiness and adversities, his intensity, his educational background, and much, much more — like I said, the sum total of all that he is.

An actor is a competent deliverer. — An actor, a good actor, not the cliché type, is in reality a "competent deliverer," one who is not just ready but artistically harmonizes this invisible duality of business and art into a successful appropriate unity. Mediocre actors or cliché actors, are plentiful but to settle down to train a "competent" actor mentally and physically is definitely not an easy task. Just as no two human beings are alike, so too with actors.

The creative restrictions of acting. — An actor is restricted. He can only do as the director instructs. In my case I can influence the production to a certain extent because of my present status. But it is not a satisfactory state of affairs because I know I am interfering and I hate to interfere with other people's work.

An actor is foremost a human being. — As far as I am concerned — and this is only my personal opinion — an actor is, first of all, like you and me, strictly a human being, and not a glamorous symbol known as a "star," which, after all, is an abstract word, a title given to you by people.

An actor is a dedicated being. — My more than twenty years experience as an actor have caused me to look at it thusly: an actor is a dedicated being who works very hard — so damn hard — that his level of understanding makes him a qualified artist in self-expression, physically, psychologically, as well as spiritually, to captivate.

Acting is honest self-expression. — One more ingredient is that an actor has to be real in expressing himself as he would honestly in a given situation. An actor's problem though is not to be egotistical and [to] keep his cool and to learn more through discoveries and much deep soul-searching. Dedication, absolute dedication is what keeps one ahead.

Creation — not imitation. A really trained, good actor is a rarity nowadays — that demands the actor to be real, to be himself. The audiences are not dumb today; an actor is not simply demonstrating what one wants others to believe he is expressing. That is mere imitation or illustration but it is not creating, even though this superficial demonstration can be "performed" with remarkable expertise.

An actor is the sum of all that he is. — Just what is an actor? Is he not the sum total of all that he is — his level of understanding, his capability to captivate the audience because he is real in the expression of his personal feelings toward what was required by the scene. You can spot such artists from ordinary ones like that. The American has a word for it, it's called *"charisma."* What you see on the screen is the sum total of his level of understanding, his taste, his educational background, his intensity.

On personal frustration in acting. — I would like to evolve into different roles, but I cannot do so in Southeast Asia. I am already typecast. I am supposed to be the good guy. I can't even be a bit gray, because no producer would let me. Besides, I can't even express myself fully on film here, or the audience wouldn't understand what I am talking about half the time.

The art of acting. — I regard acting as an art, much like my practice in martial art, because it is an expression of the self. Acting, like any profession, demands your whole-hearted devotion, no "ifs," "ands," or "buts" about it.

Business and talent. — Depending on one's level of understanding, the movie industry nowadays is basically a coexistence of practical business sense and creative talent, each being the cause and the effect of the other. To the administrators up in their administrative offices, an actor is a commodity, a product, a matter of money, money, money. "Whether or not it sells" is their chief concern. The important thing is the box-office appeal. In a way they are wrong, yet in a way they are right. I will go into that later. Though cinema is in fact a marriage of practical business and creative talent, but to regard an actor — a human being — as a product, is somewhat emotionally aggravating to me.

PART SIX

On Personal
Liberation

Conditioning

The individual and the "what should be." — Why do you as an individual depend on thousands of years of propaganda? Ideals, principles, the "what should be" leads to hypocrisy.

Be "born afresh." — Drop and dissolve inner blockage. A conditioned mind is never a free mind. Wipe away and dissolve all its experience and be "born afresh."

Keep your mind uncontaminated by past conditioning. — The more and more you're aware, the more and more you shed from day to day what you have learned so that your mind is always fresh, uncontaminated by previous conditioning.

Remove all psychic obstruction. — In order to display its native activities to the utmost limit, remove all psychic obstruction.

Drop your inner resistance. — Are you a flowing entity, capable to flow with external circumstances, or are you resisting with your set choice pattern?

The truth is outside of all set patterns. — Conditioning is to limit a person within the framework of a particular system. All fixed set patterns are incapable of adaptability or pliability. The truth is outside of all fixed patterns.

Empty your mind and expand your life. — When there is a particle of dust in your eye, the world becomes a narrow path — have your mind completely free from objects — and how much this life expands.

Live every second refreshed. — We live in clichés, in patterned behavior. We are playing the same role over and over again. To raise our potential is TO LIVE AND REVIEW EVERY SECOND REFRESHED.

One must die to one's conditioning. — One must be uninfluenced and die to one's conditioning in order to be aware of the totally fresh, totally new. Because reality changes every moment, even as I say it.

Systems

To formalize something is to make progress impossible. — Formality could be a hindrance to progress; this is applicable to everything, including philosophy. The founder of any branch must be more ingenious than the common man. However, if his achievement is not carried on by disciples of the same ingenuity, then things will only become formalized and get stuck in a cul-de-sac; whereby breakthrough and progress will be almost impossible.

The formless form. — When insubstantiality and substantiality are not set and defined, when there is no track of changing of such, one has mastered the formless form. When there is a clinging to form, when there is attachment of the mind, it is not the true path. When technique comes out of itself, it is the Way growing out of no way.

It is not simply denial. — Do not deny the classical approach as a reaction, for you will have created another pattern in which you will be trapped.

In memory of a once-fluid man. — A tombstone in memory of a man of fluidity — crammed and distorted by organized despair.

Unenlightened followers can turn truth into a tomb. — The founder [of a style or method] might have been exposed to some partial truth, but as time passed by, especially after the passing away of its founder, this partial truth became a law or, worse still, a prejudiced faith against the "different" sects. In order to pass along this knowledge from generation to generation, the various responses had to be organized and classified, and presented in a logical order. So what might have started off as some sort of personal [insight] of its founder is now solidified knowledge, a preserved cure-all for mass conditioning. In so doing, the followers have made this knowledge not only a holy shrine, but a tomb in which the founder's wisdom is buried. Because of the nature of organization and preservation, the means would become so elaborated that tremendous attention must be given to them, and gradually the end is forgotten. The followers will then accept this "organized something" as the total reality. Of course, many more "different" approaches would spring up, probably as a direct reaction to "the other's truth." Pretty soon these approaches too would become large organizations with each claiming to possess "truth" to the exclusion of all others.

The problems of belief. — Belief binds, belief isolates. An established set style. Chained down. In bondage. Bound. It can never comprehend the new, the fresh, the uncreated. The means destroys the freshness, the newness, the spontaneous discovery.

Methods block real feelings. — When real feeling occurs, like anger, fear, etc., can one "express" himself with the classical method, or is he merely listening to his own screams and yells and mechanically performing his routine?

Slaves to pattern. — Because one does not want to be disturbed, to be made uncertain, he establishes a pattern of conduct, of thought, a pattern of relationship to man, etc. Then he becomes a slave to the pattern and takes the pattern to be the real thing.

Methods place obstacles in the way of knowledge. — By an error repeated throughout the ages, truth, becoming a law or a faith, places obstacles in the way of knowledge. Method, which is in its very substance ignorance, encloses it within a vicious circle. We should break such circles not by seeking knowledge, but by discovering the cause of ignorance.

Doctrines prevent us from really seeing. — Organical seeing diminishes and evidently [is] forgotten when we begin to choose sides and set up doctrine. A path and a gateway have no meaning or use once the objective is in sight.

The nature of tradition. — Tradition equals the habit-forming mechanism of the mind.

Tradition enslaves the mind. — Classical methods and tradition make the mind a slave — you are no longer an individual, but merely a product. Your mind is the result of a thousand yesterdays.

The individual is more important than the system. — The individual is of first importance, not the system. Remember that man created method and not that method created man, and do not strain yourself in twisting into someone's preconceived pattern, which unquestionably would be appropriate for him, but not necessarily for you.

Truth is outside of all fixed patterns. — All fixed set patterns are incapable of adaptability or pliability. The truth is outside of all fixed patterns.

Freedom of expression occurs when one is beyond system. True observation begins when one is devoid of set patterns; freedom of expression occurs when one is beyond system. A style is a classified response to one's chosen inclination.

On using no way as Way — Man is constantly growing, and when he is bound by a set pattern of ideas, or "Way" of doing things, that's when he stops growing.

The limitation of having a set way of doing things. — Use no way as way. When there is a 'Way,' therein lies the limitation. And when there is a circumference, it traps. And if it traps, it rots. And if it rots, it is lifeless.

Do not restrict yourself to one approach. — There are different approaches, you know? But each person must not be limited to one approach. We must approach it with our own self—we are always in a learning process, whereas a "style" [or system] is a concluded, established, solidified something. You cannot do that, because you learn every day as you grow older.

A choice method imprisons the mind. — A choice method, however exacting, fixes the mind in a pattern. A choice method is the cultivation of resistance, and where there is resistance there is no understanding. A well-disciplined mind is not a free mind. Any technique, however worthy and desirable, becomes a disease when the mind is obsessed with it.

The creating individual is more important than any system. — Man, the living creature, the creating individual, is always more important than any established style or system.

Styles conclude, humans continue. — We are always in a learning process, whereas a "style" is a concluded, established, solidified something. You cannot do that, because you learn every day as you grow older.

The classical man is a slave to the tradition. — The classical man is just a bundle of routines, ideas, and expressed tradition. When he acts, he is translating every living moment in terms of the old.

Organized institutes produce prisoners of concepts. — I no longer am interested in systems or organization. Organized institutes tend to produce patternized prisoners of a systematized concept, and the instructors are often fixed in a routine. Of course what is worse is that by imposing the members to fit a lifeless preformation, their natural growth is blocked.

Detachment

Float in emptiness without obstruction. — The knowledge and skill you have achieved are after all meant to be "forgotten" so you can float in emptiness without obstruction and comfortably.

It is to see things as they are. — It is to see things as they are and not to become attached to anything — to be unconscious means to be innocent of the working of a relative (empirical) mind — when there is no abiding of thought anywhere on anything — this is being unbound. This not abiding anywhere is the root of our life.

Remove all psychic hindrances. — One can never be the master of his technical knowledge unless all his psychic hindrances are removed and he can keep the mind in the state of emptiness (fluidity), even purged of whatever technique he has obtained — with no conscious effort.

Emptiness cannot be confined. — You cannot hurt that which is formless. The softest thing cannot be snapped and emptiness cannot be confined.

To be detached is to be free of positive and negative. — "To desire" is an attachment. "To desire not to desire" is also an attachment. To be unattached then means to be free at once from both statements, positive and negative. In other words, this is to be simultaneously both "yes" and "no," which is intellectually absurd.

The art of detachment. — Give up thinking as though not giving it up. Observe the techniques as though not observing.

Confront the problem to be free of it. — Let yourself go with the disease, be with it, keep company with it, this is the Way to get rid of it.

The strength of emptiness. — Nothingness cannot be confined, the softest thing cannot be snapped.

Holding on prevents growth. — Tension: from NOW to THEN. People try to hold onto the sameness. This holding onto prevents growth.

No-mindedness (Wu-hsin)

No-mindedness is nonfixation. — Wu-hsin or "no-mindedness" is not a blank mind which excludes all emotions; nor is it simply callousness and quietness of mind. Although quietude and calmness are necessary, it is the "non-graspiness" of the mind that mainly constitutes the principle of "no-mindedness." The localization of the mind means its freezing. When it ceases to flow freely as it is needed, it is no more the mind in its suchness.

A mind that is not fixated is a fluid mind. — Nonfixation — a mind that has no dwelling; it doesn't stop, but continues to flow ceaselessly and ignores our limitations and our distinctions. Do not strive to localize the mind anywhere but to let it fill up the whole body; let it flow freely throughout the totality of your being. As Alan Watts puts it, the "no-mindedness" is a "state of wholeness in which the mind functions freely and easily, without the sensation of a second mind or ego standing over it with a club." What he means is to let the mind think what it likes without interference by the separate thinker or ego within oneself.

Wu-hsin is the natural process of thought. — So long as the mind thinks what it wants, there is absolutely no effort in letting it go, and the disappearance of the effort to let go is precisely the disappearance of the separate thinker. There is nothing to try to do, for whatever comes up moment by moment is accepted, including nonacceptance.

Wu-hsin is fulfillment. — "Non-seeing" and "no-mind" are not renunciations but fulfillment. The seeing that is without subject or object is "pure seeing."

No-mindedness is unobstructed feeling. — "No-mindedness" is not being without emotion or feeling, but being one in whom feeling is not sticky or blocked. It is a mind immune to emotional influences; "like this river, everything is flowing on ceaselessly without cessation or standing still." No-mindedness is to employ the whole mind as we use the eyes when we rest them upon various objects but make no special effort to take anything in.

The parable of Kwan-yin. — Kwan-yin (Avalokitesvara), the Goddess of Mercy, is sometimes represented with one thousand arms, each holding a different instrument. If her mind stops with the use, for instance, of a spear, all the other arms (999) will be of no use whatever. It is only because of her mind not stopping with the use of one arm, but moving from one instrument to another, that all her arms prove useful with the utmost degree of efficiency. Thus the figure is meant to demonstrate that, when the ultimate truth is realized, even as many as one thousand arms on one body may each be serviceable in one way or another.

Wu-hsin is making oneself empty. — I must give up my desire to force, direct, strangle the world outside of me and within me in order to be completely open, responsible, aware, alive. This is often called "to make oneself empty" — which does not mean something negative, but means the openness to receive.

Wu-hsin is the fluidity of "everyday mind." — This "non-stopping" mind is known as fluidity, which is also known as the "empty mind" or " everday mind." To have something in mind means that it is preoccupied and has no time for anything else. But to attempt to remove the thought already in it is to refill it with another something. So what to do! Do nothing! Don't solve it, dissolve it — not fuss, no fuss — it's the everyday mind, nothing special at all.

Zen Buddhism

Zen has no metaphysics. — Zen wishes to escape the pointless endeavor to trap life in a metaphysical net instead of simply living it.

Zen reveals that there is no problem — and no solution. — Zen reveals that there is no where for man to go out of this world; no tavern in which he can overcome anxiety; no jail in which he can expiate guilt. So, instead of telling us what the problem is, Zen insists that the whole trouble is just our failure to realize that there is no problem. And, of course, this means that there is no solution, either.

The parable of a tea serving. — A learned man once went to a Zen master to inquire about Zen. As the Zen master talked, the learned man would frequently interrupt him with remarks like, "Oh yes, we have too," etc. Finally the Zen master stopped talking and began to serve tea to the learned man; however, he kept on pouring until the tea cup overflowed. "Enough, no more can go into the cup!" the learned man interrupted. "Indeed I see," answered the Zen master. "But if you do not first empty your cup, then how can you taste my cup of tea?"

Buddhism is effortless. — In Buddhism there is no place for using effort. Just be ordinary and nothing special. Eat your food, move your bowels, pass water, and when you're tired go and lie down. The ignorant will laugh at me, but the wise will understand.

On Buddhism's Eight-Fold Path. — The eight requirements that will eliminate suffering by correcting false values and giving true knowledge of life's meaning have been summed up as follows:

- First, you must see clearly what is wrong.

- Next, decide to be cured.

- You must act.

- Speak so as to aim at being cured.

- Your livelihood must not conflict with your therapy.

- The therapy must go forward at the "staying speed;" the critical velocity that can be sustained.

- You must think and feel about it incessantly.

- Learn how to contemplate with the deep mind.

OR

- Right views (or understanding).

- Right purpose (or aspiration).

- Right speech.

- Right conduct.

- Right means of livelihood (or vocation).

- [Right effort.]

- Right kind of awareness or mind control.

- Right concentration or meditation.

Zen has no idols. — Zen liberates the mind from servitude to imagined spiritual states as "objects," which too easily become hypostatized and turn into idols that obsess and delude the seeker.

Transcending karma. — The way to transcend Karma lies in the proper use of the mind and the will.

The Zen of assertion. — An assertion is Zen only when it is itself an act and does not refer to anything that is asserted
in it.

On prajna (wisdom). — Prajna is not self-realization, but realization pure and simple, beyond subject and object.

On the bodhisattva. — Leaving sagehood behind and entering once more into ordinary humanity. After coming to understand the other side, you come back and live on this side.

Meditation

Meditation is not introversion. — It is not a technique of introversion by which one seeks to exclude matter and the external world, to eliminate distracting thoughts, to sit in silence emptying the mind of images, and to concentrate on the purity of one's own spiritual essence. Zen is not a mysticism of "introversion" and "withdrawal." It is not "acquired contemplation." To think that this insight is a subjective experience "attainable" by some kind of process of mental purification is to doom oneself to error and absurdity — "mirror-wiping Zen."

Stop inwardly. — At this moment stop inwardly — when you do stop inwardly, psychologically, your mind becomes very peaceful, very clear. Then you can really look at "this."

Meditation is enlightenment. — Do not separate meditation as a means (dhyana) from enlightenment as an end (Prajana) — the two were really inseparable, and the Zen discipline consisted in seeking to realize this wholeness and unity of prajna and dhyana in all one's acts.

Enlightenment is knowledge. — There is no difference between such enlightenment and what is ordinarily termed knowledge, for in the latter a contrast exists between the knower and the known, whereas in the former there can be no such contrast.

Meditation leads to thought that is not of the physical. — After the completion of cultivation (of no cultivation), one's thoughts continue to be detached from phenomenal things, and one still remains amid the phenomenal yet devoid of the phenomenal.

Real meditation puts you in the Now. — Zen is not "attained" by mirror-wiping meditation, but by "self-forgetfulness in the existential 'present' of life here and now." We do not "come," we "are." Don't strive to become, but be.

Meditation is without motive. — A simple mind, surely, is one that functions, that thinks and feels without a motive. Where there is a motive, there must be a way, a method, a system of discipline. The motive is brought about by the desire for an end, for a goal, and to achieve that goal there must be a way, etc. Meditation is a freeing of the mind from all motives.

Meditation is without mental effort. — Any effort the mind makes will further limit the mind, because effort implies the struggle towards a goal, and when you have a goal, a purpose, an end in view, you have placed a limit on the mind, and it is with such a mind that you are trying to meditate.

Meditation is not concentration. — Meditation, surely, can never be a process of concentration, because the highest form of thinking is negative thinking. Negation is not the opposite of positive, but a state in which there is neither the positive nor its reaction as the negative. It is a state of complete emptiness.

Meditation means to be internally unperturbed. — To meditate means to realize the imperturbability of one's original nature. Meditation means to be free from all phenomena, and calmness means to be internally unperturbed. There will be calmness when one is free from external objects and is not perturbed.

On Being Centered

Hold to the core. — We are vortices whose center is a point that is motionless and eternal but which appears in manifestation as motion which increases in velocity in the manner of a whirlpool or tornado (whose epicenter is still) from nucleus to periphery. The nucleus is in Reality, whereas the vortex is phenomenon in the form of a multidimensional force field — HOLD TO THE CORE.

The immovable. — The immovable — it is the concentration of energy at a given focus — as at the axis of a wheel — instead of dispersal in scattered activities.

Stillness in motion. — I'm moving and not moving at all. I'm like the moon underneath the waves that ever go on rolling and rocking.

Freedom

Where method is, freedom is not. — The more complicated and restricted the method, the lesser the opportunity for the expression of one's original sense of freedom.

Freedom cannot be preconceived. — Freedom is something that cannot be preconcieved. To realize freedom requires an alert mind, a mind that is deep with energy, a mind that is capable of immediate perception without the process of graduation, without the idea of an end to be slowly achieved. Preformations simply lack the flexibility to adapt to the ever-changing. At this point, many would ask "how then do we gain this unlimited freedom?" I cannot tell you because it will then become an approach. Although I can tell you what is not, I cannot tell you what is. "That," my friend, you will have to find out all by yourself, for there is no help but self-help.

On "gaining" freedom. — Who says we have to "gain" freedom? Freedom has always been with us and [is] not something to be gained at the end through following some particular formulas. We do not "become," we simply "are."

On being free. — Free equals the absence of feeling of external constraint. Not free equals the absence of presence of the feeling of external constraint. Different people feel free in different ways. Therefore, it is in degree. The question should then be "how free are we?"

On freeing oneself. — To free yourself, observe closely what you normally practice. Do not condemn or approve, merely observe.

To express in freedom. — To express yourself in freedom, you must die to everything of yesterday. If you follow the classical pattern, you're not understanding the routines, the traditions; you are not understanding yourself.

Things that limit freedom. — There is no freedom if you are enclosed by:

· Self-interest

· Walls of discipline

The relationship of freedom to sensitivity. — Great freedom = great sensitivity.

Understand this freedom: The freedom from the conformity of styles.

Personal expression must be free. — Expression must be free. This liberating truth becomes reality only in proportion to its being experienced and lived in its suchness by the individual himself.

The three keys. — Simplicity. Directness. Freedom.

Freedom knows no past. — To express yourself in freedom, you must die to everything of yesterday.

Beyond right and wrong. — There is no such thing as doing right or wrong when there is freedom.

Freedom and intelligence. — Real freedom is the outcome of intelligence.

Freedom is self-knowledge. — Freedom lies in understanding yourself from moment to moment.

PART SEVEN

The Process
of Becoming

Self-actualization

The second-hand artist (the conformer). — The second-hand artist, in blindly following the teacher, accepts his pattern and, as a result, his action and, above all, his thinking becomes mechanical, his responses automatic according to the pattern — and thereby he ceases to expand or to grow. He is a mechanical robot, a product of thousands of years of propaganda and conditioning. The second-hand artist seldom learns to depend upon himself for expression; instead, he faithfully follows an imposed pattern. So what is nurtured is the dependent mind rather than independent inquiry.

The "Mirror Person." — A mirror-person is one who always wants to know how he looks to others. Instead of being critical, he projects the criticism and feels criticized and feels onstage.

The most poignant sense of insecurity comes from standing alone. — We [tend to] have more faith in what we imitate than in what we originate. We [often feel that we] cannot derive a sense of absolute certitude from anything which has its root in us. The most poignant sense of insecurity comes from standing alone; we are not alone when we imitate.

Do not look for a successful personality to duplicate. — When I look around, I always learn something and that is *to be always yourself.* And to express yourself. To have faith in yourself. Do not go out and look for a successful personality and duplicate it, which seems to me to be the prevalent thing happening in Hong Kong. Like they always copy mannerisms, but they'll never start from the very root of his being, which is *"how can I be me?"*

The need to be real. — In life, what more can you ask for but to be real? To fulfill one's potential instead of wasting energy on actualizing one's dissipating image, which is not real, and the expenditure of one's vital energy. We have great work ahead of us, and it needs devotion and much, much energy.

Perform your own mission in life. — If you look within yourself and are sure that you have done right, what do you have to fear or worry about? You are required only to perform your own mission in life without any thoughts of aggressiveness or competition.

Most of us see ourselves as instruments in the hands of others. — There is a powerful craving in most of us to see ourselves as instruments in hands of others and thus free ourselves from the responsibility for acts which are prompted by our own questionable inclinations and impulses. Both the strong and the weak grasp at this alibi. The latter hide their malevolence under the virtue of obedience: they acted dishonorably because they had to obey orders. The strong, too, claim absolution by proclaiming themselves the chosen instrument of a higher power — God, history, fate, nation, or humanity.

Self-actualization is the highest state. — This achieving the center, being grounded in one's self, is about the highest state a human being can achieve.

Strive to be better. — One must always strive to be better. The sky's the limit.

To find the Way. — To be on the alert means to be deadly serious, to be deadly serious means to be sincere to oneself, and it is sincerity that finally leads one to discover the *Way.*

On the light within. — No matter what, you must let your inner light guide you out of the darkness.

Ignorance is blind. — Those who are unaware they are walking in darkness will never seek the light.

The process of self-cultivation. — Wishing to cultivate oneself, one first rectifies his heart (mind). Wishing to rectify his heart, one seeks to be sincere in his thoughts. Wishing to be sincere in his thoughts, one first extends to the utmost of his knowledge — such extension of knowledge lies in the investigation of things.

The statement of the self-actualized. — I am what I am here and now.

Self-actualization vs. self-image actualization. — Yes, there is a difference between self-actualization and self-image actualization. Most people only live for their image, that is why where some have a self, a starting point, most people have a void, because they are so busy projecting themselves as this or that, dedicating their lives to actualize a *concept* of what they should be like rather than to actualize their ever-growing potentiality as a human being. Wasting, dissipating all their energy in projection and conjuring up of facade, rather than centering their energy on expanding and broadening their potential or expressing and relaying this unified energy for efficient communication, etc.

Maintaining a facade is futile. — The futility of maintaining a facade to act in one way on the surface when actually experiencing something quite different. Being one's self leads to real relationships, and the acceptance of self leads to change.

A self-actualizing person is a real person. — When a [self-actualizing] human being sees another self-actualizing person walk past, he cannot help but say *"hey, now there is someone real!"*

How one becomes what one is. — Self-actualization is the important thing. And my personal message to people is that I hope they will go towards self-actualization rather than self-image actualization. I hope that they will search within themselves for honest self-expression.

Absorb what is useful. — Research your own experience; absorb what is useful, reject what is useless and add what is essentially your own.

True individualism is self-sufficiency. — Evaluation by others is not a guide for me. Only the self-sufficient stand alone — most people follow the crowd and imitate.

The self-actualized seek freedom and purity. — Those who distrust the life-giving force within them, or who have none, are driven to compensate through such substitutes as money. When a man has confidence in himself, when all he wants in the world is to live out his destiny in freedom and purity, he comes to regard all those vastly overestimated and far too costly possessions as mere accessories, pleasant perhaps to have and make use of, but never essential.

To actualize one must listen. — Stop wasting time in playing a role or a concept. Instead, learn to ACTUALIZE yourself, your potential. The main thing is to listen. To listen, to understand, to be open, is one and the same.

The path of self-realization is the most difficult. — We acquire a sense of worth either by realizing our talents, or by keeping busy, or by identifying ourselves with something apart from us — be it a cause, a leader, a group, possessions, and the like. Of the three, the path of self-realization is the most difficult. It is taken when other avenues to a sense of worth are more or less blocked.

Self-realization is enlightenment. — *Satori,* in the awakening from a dream. Awakening and self-realization and seeing into one's own being — these are synonymous.

The sacred journey is taken alone. — Each man must seek out realization himself. No master can give it to him.

The image creates dependency. — If you disown yourself to play an image [concept of yourself], you will become the target, you will become dependent.

Playing the concept wastes valuable energy. — Playing the *concept* strengthens our negativeness, prevents us from seeing, and, above all, wastes a lot energy, instead of using this energy creatively for our own development.

Be alert, question and find out. — The important thing for you is to be alert, to question, to find out, so that your own initiative may be awakened.

Self-help

There is only self-help. — I have come to discover through earnest personal experience and dedicated learning that ultimately the greatest help is self-help; that there is no other help but self-help — doing one's best, dedicating one's self whole-heartedly to a given task, which happens to have no end but is an ongoing process.

Admitting mistakes. — Mistakes are always forgivable, if one has the courage to admit them.

There is no external help. — The problem lies in asking somebody else to solve your own problem instead of asking yourself. I can give you ten thousand of my ways, but they are *my* way, not yours. An individual's questions are answerable only by the individual himself, and nothing would be gained by his sitting in on a recital of mine (pause).

The medicine for suffering is within. — The medicine for my suffering I had within me from the very beginning, but I did not take it. My ailment came from within myself, but I did not observe it — until this moment. Now I see that I will never find the light unless, like the candle, I am my own fuel, consuming myself.

Self-help comes in many forms. — Self-help comes in many forms: daily discoveries through choiceless observation, honesty, as we always whole-heartedly do our best, a sort of indomitable, obsessive dedication, and above all, to realize that there is no end or limit to this, because life is simply an *ever-going process.*

The key to liberation is within. — Each man binds himself; the fetters are ignorance, laziness, preoccupation with self, and fear. He must liberate himself, while accepting the fact that we are of this world, so that "In summer we sweat; in winter we shiver."

Self-reliance. — Self-reliance — find your own need, your own qualification.

To conquer oneself. — A man is born to achieve great things if he has the strength to conquer himself. To see oneself is to be clear of right.

Unfinished situations. — We carry much of the past with us only as far as we have UNFINISHED SITUATIONS.

The greatest victory is over oneself. — Self-conquest is the greatest of victories. Mighty is he who conquers himself.

Learn your nature in order to control it. — In order to control myself I must first accept myself by going with and not against my nature. Everybody has to think for himself. A right way for a big man may not be a right way for a small man. A right way for someone who is slow may not be a right way for someone who is quick. Each person must understand his weaknesses and his strengths.

Self-knowledge

Know thyself. — It is later than you think! Know yourself!!

The answer within. — Instead of establishing rigid rules and separative thoughts, we should look within ourselves to see where our particular problems lie and our cause of ignorance. You see, ultimately, all type of knowledge simply means self-knowledge. You must look for the truth yourself and directly experience every minute detail for yourself.

Self-knowledge involves relationship. — To know oneself is to study oneself in action with another person. Relationship is a process of self-revelation. Relationship is the mirror in which you discover yourself — to be is to be related.

The liberating quality of self-knowledge. — When you're faced with looking at your own life with awakened eyes, you will have increased a bit in the knowledge of yourself (in other words, your mental and physical abilities will become clear to you), and knowledge of anything outside of yourself is only superficial and very shallow. To put it another way, self knowledge has a liberating quality.

Man at his worst. — A man is at his worst when he does not understand himself. When I first arrived I did "The Green Hornet" television series back in 1965. And, as I looked around, man, I saw a lot of human beings. And as I looked at myself I was the only robot there. Because I was not being myself, and I was trying to accumulate external securities. External technique; the way to move my arm, the way to move — but never to ask and learn what would Bruce Lee have done if — the word "if" — such a thing had happened to me?

Criticizing others is easier than coming to know yourself. — For it is easy to criticize and break down the spirit of others, but to know yourself takes maybe a lifetime. To take responsibility of one's actions, good and bad, is something else. After all, all knowledge simply means self-knowledge.

The continuous peeling of self. — My life it seems is a life of self-examination: a self-peeling of my self, bit by bit, day by day. More and more it's becoming simple to me as a human being [as] more and more I search [within] myself. And more and more the questions become listed. And more and more I see clearly. It is not a question of developing what has already been developed but of recovering what has been left behind. Though this has been with us, in us, all the time and has never been lost or distorted except for our misguided manipulation of it.

The need to question. — Oh I know we all admit that we are intelligent beings; yet, I wonder how many of us have gone through some sort of self-inquiries and/or self-examining of all these ready-made facts or truths that are crammed down our throats ever since we acquired the capacity and the sensibility to learn.

Learning to truly see. — We possess a pair of eyes, but most of us do not really see in the true sense of the word. I must say that when the eyes are used externally to observe the inevitable faults of other beings, most of us are rather quick with readily-equipped condemnation. True seeing, in the sense of choiceless awareness, leads to new discovery, and discovery is one of the means to uncovering our potentiality.

Look for your resentment. — If you have any difficulties in communication with somebody, look for your resentment. Whenever you feel guilty, find out what you are resenting and express it and make your demand explicit.

Self-knowledge as the road to freedom. — Freedom lies in understanding yourself from moment to moment.

Attend to the inner self. — The pursuit of pleasures deranges the mind of man. The love for wealth perverts the conduct of man. Therefore the Sage attends to the Inner Self, and not to the outward appearance.

Self-knowledge and intelligence. — Intelligence is the understanding of self.

Awareness vs. robotics. — Be "self-aware" rather than [a] repetitious robot.

The transcendence. — I have changed from self-image actualization to self-actualization, from blindly following propaganda, organized truths, etc., to search internally for the cause of my ignorance.

Public esteem vs. self-esteem. — Esteem by others or self-esteem, which is better? To value things or to value yourself, which is better? To have more or to have less, which is worse? The more you have, the more you have to lose. The more you value things, the less you value yourself. The more you depend upon others for esteem, the less you are self-sufficient.

Self-knowledge is true mastery. — True mastery transcends any particular art. It stems from mastery of oneself — the ability, developed through self-discipline to be calm, fully aware, and completely in tune with oneself and the surroundings. Then, and only then, can a person know himself.

Self-knowledge is the task of the living. — While we are still alive, we have to discover ourselves, understand ourselves, and express ourselves.

Self-expression

Head toward self-expression. — Head toward self-expression and self-actualization and not just a means of mediocre functioning or repetitious drilling on a chosen pattern.

The importance of self-expression. — Self-expression is important. Only the self-sufficient stand alone — most people follow the crowd and imitate.

Express the truth of your vision. — One must not merely copy but try to convey the significance of what you see.

Self-expression makes for true relationships. — To be neither occult nor complex, but open and simple. Thus being one's true, open self leads to true relationship.

Towards self-expression. — The only way toward self-expression is totally, immediately, without time, and you can express yourself thus when you are not fragmented, physically or mentally.

Honest self-expression is difficult. — To express oneself honestly, not lying to oneself; that, my friend, is very hard to do.

Self-expression is the response to what is. — When one is not "expressing" himself, he is not free. Thus he begins to struggle, and the struggle breeds methodical routine. Pretty soon one is doing his methodical routine as response rather than responding to what is.

On Growth

Personal growth. — Growth is getting through role-playing and filling in the holes in the personality to make the person whole and complete again.

Growth requires involvement. — To grow, to discover, we need involvement which is something I experience everyday, sometimes good, sometimes frustrating.

Awareness of "now" and "how." — Anytime you use the words NOW and HOW and become aware of this, you grow — it's the remedy of reintegrating, taking back what is rightfully yours.

The nature of growth. — Growth is the constant discovery and understanding in one's process of living.

Learning is boundless. — I dare not say that I have reached any state of achievement. I'm still learning, for learning is boundless.

The need to progress. — Do not hold to what you have. It is like a ferry boat for people who want to get across waters. Once you have got across, never bear it on your back. You should head forward.

Discovery + understanding = growth + learning. — Daily discovery and understanding is the process of growth and learning. I am happy because I am growing daily and honestly don't know where my ultimate limit lies. To be certain, every day there can be a revelation or a new discovery that I can obtain.

The need to make new discoveries every day. — I am improving and making new discoveries every day. If you don't you are already crystallized and that's it.

Maturity vs. maturing. — There is no such word as "maturity." Rather: matur*ing*. Because when there is a maturity, there is a conclusion and a cessation. That's "the end." That's when the coffin is closed.

On maturing. — To mature means to take responsibility for your life and to be on your own. *Maturing* is the transcendence from environmental support to self-support.

Growth is constant. — Man is constantly growing. And when he is bound by a set pattern of ideas, or "Way" of doing things, that's when he stops growing.

Age and discovery. — You might be deteriorating, physically, in the long process of aging, but in your daily discovery, it's still the very same every day. You do not get better as you grow older — you only get wiser.

To understand is to connect. — The more we understand, the greater and deeper will be our contact with all that is around us.

The growth aim. — The growth aim is to lose more and more of your "mind" and come more to your sense. To be more and more in touch with yourself and the world, instead of only in touch with the fantasies, prejudices, etc.

Frustration is a means of growth. — People have to grow by skillful frustrations, otherwise they have no incentive to develop their own means and ways of coping with the world.

Growth as a result of contrast. — In the contrast of comparison some new thing might grow.

Mistakes as educators. — When I have listened to my mistakes, I have grown.

Simplicity

Profound simplicity = common sense. — A profound simplicity of common sense; the straightest, most logical way.

True refinement seeks simplicity. — The height of cultivation runs to simplicity. Halfway cultivation runs to ornamentation.

The way of the simpleton. A simpleton: lays down no first law, takes everything that happens as it comes. The simplicity of the truly sophisticated

Simplicity is the result of profound cultivation. — Simplicity — the natural result of profound cultivation. The mark of genius is the capacity to see and to express what is simple, simply! The really great Zen artist states the utmost in the minimum of lines or effort.

Simplicity is hacking away the unessential. — It is not daily increase but daily decrease — hack away the unessential! The closer to the source, the less wastage there is.

The semi-actualized talk to impress. — False teachers of the Way of life use flowery words.

Simplicity is difficult. — It is indeed difficult to convey simplicity.

Simplicity is an inward state. — Simplicity is an inward state of being in which there is no contradiction, no comparison; it is the quality of perception in approaching any problem — it is not simply when the mind approaches any problem with a fixed idea of belief, or with a particular pattern of thought.

Simplicity is the natural way. — The natural way is compared with the ways of water. The female and the infant, that is the way of the weak. While there seems to be glorification of the weak, the strongest stress really lies with "simplicity."

PART EIGHT

On Ultimate (Final) Principles

Yin-yang

On yin-yang. — Yin and yang are two interlocking parts of one whole, each containing within its confines the qualities of its complementaries. Etymologically, the two characters of yin and yang mean darkness and light.

The etymology of yang. — The yang (whiteness) principle represents positiveness, firmness, masculinity, substantiality, brightness, day, heat, etc.

The etymology of yin. — The yin (blackness) principle represents negativeness, softness, femininity, insubstantiality, darkness, night, coldness, and so forth.

The basic theory underlying yin-yang. — The basic theory in yin-yang is that nothing is so permanent as never to change. In other words, when activity (yang) reaches the extreme point, it becomes inactivity, and inactivity forms yin. Extreme inactivity will, in the same way, return to become activity, which is yang. Activity then is the cause of inactivity, and vice versa. This system of complementary increasing and decreasing of the principle is continuous. From this, one can see that the two forces (yin-yang), although they appear to conflict, in reality are mutually interdependent; instead of opposition, there is cooperation and alternation.

Yin-yang is not dualistic. — The common mistake of the Western World is to identify these two forces, yin and yang, as dualistic; that is, yang being the opposite of yin, and vice versa. At best they see the two forces as cause and effect, but never paired like sound and echo, or light and shadow.

Yin-yang — not yin and *yang.* — You cannot use the word "and" when speaking of yin-yang, as yin-yang is never two, but rather poles of one interconnected process. Just as in pedaling a bicycle; you cannot just push or not push; unless both legs are working together, you cannot get anywhere. Neither can be omitted or separate from the other. Why do we have to use this kind of thinking? It's like trying to move an elephant by pulling it — very unnatural. We must follow the natural course, just like the up and down of pedaling a bicycle. If you tried to pedal by just pushing — or by just releasing — you would get nowhere and would never get to enjoy the beauty of the scenery outdoors.

On the balance inherent in yin-yang. — In the yin-yang symbol there is a white spot on the black part and a black spot on the white one. This is to illustrate the balance in life, for nothing can survive long going to either extreme, be it pure yin (mere passiveness) or pure yang (mere activeness). Notice the stiffest tree is most easily cracked, while the bamboo or willow survive by bending with the wind. Extreme heat kills and so does extreme cold; no violent extremes can endure long, but a sober moderation [can]. Therefore positiveness (yang) should be concealed in negativeness (yin), and vice versa.

K'un (yin) is the perfect complement to ch'ien (yang). — K'un (yin, the receptive) is the perfect complement of the ch'ien (yang, the positive) — the complement, not the opposite, for the receptive does not combat the positive (ch'ien) but completes it. The receptive must be activated and led by the positive (ch'ien). Only when it abandons this position and tries to stand as an equal side by side with the positive, does it become evil. Each is the cause and result of one another. The result then is opposition to and struggle against the positive, which is evil. It is the positive that begets things, but they're brought to birth by the receptive. The receptive accommodates itself to the qualities of the positive and makes them its own. Therefore the receptive has no need of a special purpose of its own, nor of any effort; yet everything turns out as it should. The yin opens when it moves and closes when at rest. Be soft yet not yielding; firm, yet not hard.

On Zen and yin-yang. — Zen has derived many of its concepts from the Chinese belief in balance: yin, which is feminine and gentle, and yang, which is masculine and firm. Having accepted that basic idea, another must be added: there is no such thing as pure yin or pure yang. Gentleness should cloak firmness; firmness should be modified by gentleness.

Yin-yang and the relationship of good and bad. — Good and bad or pleasure and pain exist but for the other. Instead of opposites, they are complementaries and [each] is a function each of the other. First of all, if I have not felt pain how can I distinguish pleasure, or vice versa? Looking at the sky I can distinguish a smaller star because of the big stars, and, if there were no black sky at all, there will be no stars. It is not a matter to struggle between the good and the bad, but to flow like waves on the water.

The way of yin-yang. — When one wishes to expand, one must first contract. When one wishes to be strong, one must first be weak. When one wishes to take, one must first give. Everything in this world has the alternative of existence and nonexistence (positive and negative)

Yin-yang and its relationship to Eastern and Western culture. — Nothing is superior in every respect. The Occidental education is excellent in some ways, the Oriental in others. You will say, "This finger is better for one purpose; this finger is better for another." But the entire hand is better for all purposes. There are good points in Chinese culture; there are good points in Occidental culture. Oriental culture and Occidental culture are not mutually exclusive, but mutually dependent. Neither would be remarkable if it were not for the existence of the other.

Yin-yang and its relationship to man and woman. — No woman should follow passively. She must learn that there is an active way of following. She must have what the Occidentals call "backbone." By the same reasoning, no man should be totally firm; his resolve must be softened by compassion.

Yin-yang represents totality. — In reality, things are whole and cannot be separated into two parts. When I say "the heat makes me perspire," the heat and perspiring are just one process as they are coexistent, and the one could not exist but for the other. Just as an object needs a subject, a person in question is not taking an independent position but is acting as an assistant. Things do have their complementaries, and complementaries coexist; instead of [being] mutually exclusive, they are mutually dependent and are a function each of the other. No part has a life of its own, but each exists in complementary interaction WITH the other. Yin and yang mutually help each other — duality in harmonious relationship.

Yin-yang and extremes in trends. — Nothing can be secured by extremes. For instance, the haircuts worn by many boys at this time are not haircuts at all, but disguises. The fashion cannot last, because it is extreme and will soon tire the wearer and the beholder. Possibly the beholder more quickly, but a vast boredom for all in any case. The so-called jet set is really boring to that extent that they all go to extremes.

Yin-yang and chatterboxes. — The more volubly one talks, the quicker will come his exhaustion.

Totality

Do not cling to partiality. — Do not cling to partiality, however fantastic — see things from TOTALITY.

Be affected by the totality of creative energy. — Move "playfully serious" from the creative tide (primordial creative energy) affected by it totally and not a mere fragment.

Totality and enlightenment. — To obtain enlightenment means the extinction of everything which obscures the "true knowledge," the "real life;" at the same time, it implies "boundless expansion," and, indeed emphasis should fall not on the cultivation of the "particular department which merges into the totality," but rather on "the totality that enters and unites that particular department!"

There is no effective segment of a totality. — There is no such thing as an effective segment of a totality. How can one respond to the totality with [a] partial, fragmentary pattern? In the greater the lesser is, but in the lesser the greater is not.

The way to freedom is through totality. — Fluidity leads to interchangeability. Self-knowledge leads to awareness. Totality leads to ultimate freedom.

Beyond liking and disliking. — You will then see it without like or dislike, you simply see, and in this seeing, the whole is presented and not the partial.

Do not be anchored to one view. — Having the totality means capable of following with what is, because what is *is* constantly moving and constantly changing, and if one is anchored down to one partialized view, one will not be able to follow the swift movement of what is.

Totality in action. — Action is not a matter or right and wrong. It is only when action is partial, not total, that there is right and wrong.

To be whole. — An organism works as a whole. We are not a summation of part, but a very subtle *coordination* of all these different bits that go into the making of the organism — we *HAVE* not a liver or a heart. We *ARE* liver and heart and brain and so on.

On viewing totality. — To view totality one has to be a total outsider.

Tao

The history of Tao. — To the Chinese what is highest, the origin of things, is nothingness, emptiness, the altogether undetermined, the abstract universal, and this is also called Tao. Before Confucius, the term "Tao" usually meant a road, or a way of action. Confucius used it as a philosophical concept standing for the right way of action — moral, social, and political. The Taoist used the term "Tao" to stand for the totality of all things, equivalent to what some philosophers* have called "The Absolute." The "Tao" was the basic stuff out of which all things were made. It was simple, formless, desireless, without striving, supremely content.

Gentleness in the Tao Te Ching. — In *Tao Te Ching*, the gospel of Taoism, Lao-tzu pointed out to us the value of gentleness. Contrary to common belief, the yin principle, as softness and pliableness, is to be associated with life and survival. Because he can yield, a man can survive. In contrast, the yang principle, which is assumed to be rigorous and hard, makes a man break under pressure.

* [i.e., Hegel]

On uniting with Tao — a personal experience. — I lay on the boat and felt that I had united with Tao; I had become one with nature. I just lay there and let the boat drift freely according to its own will. For at that moment I had achieved a state of inner feeling in which opposition had become mutually cooperative instead of mutually exclusive, in which there was no longer any conflict in my mind. The whole world to me was unitary.

The Tao and emptiness. — The assimilation of the Tao has its foundation in "meekness," "tenderness," poverty of spirit, and quietness. These are expressed sometimes by one word, "emptiness." An aggressive spirit will be brought low, pride leads to a fall, violence will end in defeat, all [of] which come from misunderstanding the real use of Tao.

The philosophy of Taoism. — Taoism is a philosophy of the essential unity of the universe (monism), or reversion, polarization (yin & yang), and eternal cycles, of the leveling of all differences, the relativity of all standards, and the return of all to the primeval one, the divine intelligence, the source of all things. From this naturally arises the absence of desire for strife and contention and fighting for advantage. Thus the teachings of humility and meekness of the Christian Sermon on the Mount find a rational basis, and a peaceable temper is bred in man. It emphasizes nonresistance and the importance of gentleness.

Tao is truth. — The word "Tao" has no exact equivalent in the English language. To render it into "Way," "Principle," or "Law" is to give it a too narrow interpretation. Although no one word can substitute [for] it's meaning, I have used the word "Truth" for it.

Truth

To be truthful and honest. — One must be truthful and honest in his approach; a constant independent inquiry and not blindly following a certain blue print laid down by others.

Truth is where the problem is. — We shall find the truth when we examine the problem. The problem is never apart from the answer, the problem *is* the answer — the understanding of the problem is the dissolution of the problem. It is a mistake to think that one can establish a universal definition for verification.

Determining truth in propositions. — A proposition is true if:

· Every proposition corresponds to a fact in the world.

· Every proposition is a kind of symbol which pictures a particular fact — e.g., musical scales. If a picture is true, therefore a proposition is true.

· Indefinable view

· Coherence view

· Every proposition should fit into and will not contradict the set.

· Cannot dissect experience into subject and predicate

· Can take experience as a whole

· Reality is coherent.

Determining truth in statements. — A statement of reality is true if it doesn't contradict other statements concerning reality.

Determining truth in beliefs. — A belief is true if and only if one can act on it without upsetting one's expectation.

Truth in nature. — There is an element of truth in everything. Nature teaches, although it can sometimes be misleading.

The man who seeks truth lives in what is. — The man who is really serious, with the urge to find out what truth is, has not style at all. He lives only in what is.

Truth must be experienced by the individual to be meaningful. — A fat belly cannot believe that such a thing as hunger exists. It is something you have to go through and understand. No one can eat and digest your food for you in order to give you the necessary strength to live.

The realization of truth. — Truth comes when your mind and heart are purged of all sense of striving and you are no longer trying to become somebody; it is there when the mind is very quiet, listening timelessly to everything.

The paradigm of truth. — I have said before "truth is nowhere to be found on a map." Your truth is different from that of mine. At first, you may think that this is truth, but later you discover another truth, and then the former truth is denied — but you are closer to truth. Perhaps when we have found out more about what is *not* the truth, we will be that much closer to the truth. To experience pain, for example, does not necessarily mean that one understands it, accepts it, or even for that matter, denies its existence: It *is*. But it does not follow that everyone will understand pain in the same way and arrive at the same conclusion. All one has to do is take a close look at the medical profession. However, when I say that pain "is," [this] does imply that I am experiencing some THING, but to relate this THING to someone other than myself seems to be where the difficulty lies. It is, I believe, more than a semantic difficulty — it is an impossibility. Semantically, we all respond to a given idea, concept, or word in much the same way: that is, if the concept, idea, or word is in our own native language.

Truth cannot be limited. — Truth cannot be structured or confined. When there is no center and no circumference, then there is truth.

Truth cannot be organized. — You can't organize truth. That's like trying to put a pound of water into wrapping paper and shaping it.

School yourself in the truth. — Cultivate and school yourself in the TRUTH — study hard and enjoy your planning and steps to ultimate fulfillment. Partialized cultivation is not an approach to truth; there is no "your style" or "my style," but only the intelligent understanding of the problem.

The ways of truth. — The ways of truth consist of seeking after truth, awareness of truth (and it's existence), perception of truth (it's substance and direction, like the perception of movement), understanding of truth, experiencing of truth, mastering of truth, forgetting truth, forgetting the carrier of truth, the return to the primal source where truth has its roots, and repose in nothing.

First-rate philosophers practice truth in order to understand it. — According to Tao, a first-rate philosopher practices truth in order to understand it. Krishnamurti pointed out that in order to see truth, one cannot be fragmented, but must see the totality.

On being truthful. — If you don't want to slip up tomorrow, speak the truth today.

Truth is everyday life. — The truth and the *Way* exhibit in the simple everyday movements. Because of this, many miss it (if there is any secret, it is missed by seeking). If there is any secret, one must have lost it by striving for it. The truth is here but men want to decorate the simple truth — the snake with feet.

Truth as liberating agent. — The direct awareness in which is formed "truth that makes us free" — not the truth as an object of knowledge, only but the truth lived and experienced in concrete and existential awareness.

Anger and truth. — That man in whom the truth is bright has no anger.

Truth transcends "for" and "against." — The perfect Way is only difficult for those who pick and choose; do not like, do not dislike; all will then be clear. Make a hair's-breadth difference, and heaven and earth are set apart; if you want the truth to stand clear before you, never be for or against. The struggle between "for" and "against" is the mind's worst disease.

One's perspective on truth changes with change. — Because I am a changing as well as an ever-growing man, thus what I hold true a couple of months ago might not be the same now.

There is a pathless road. — Truth is a pathless road. A road that is not a road. It is total expression that has no before or after. How can there be methods and systems by which to arrive at something that is living? To that which is static, fixed, dead, there can be a way, a definite path, but not to that which is living.

Truth is outside molds and patterns. — Truth exists outside of all molds and patterns, and awareness is never exclusive. Truth is never a set idea and definitely not a conclusion. Styles and methods are conclusions but the truth of life is a process.

Find out for yourself what is true. — Create immediately an atmosphere of freedom so that you can live and find out for yourselves what is true, so that you are able to face the world with the ability to understand it, not just conform to it. One can tell for oneself whether the water is warm or cold. In the same way, a man must convince himself about these experiences, only then are they real.

Discard what is ornamental. — Shun what is trivial and discard what is ornamental.

The ultimate truth. — The ultimate has no symbol, no style, no superhuman.

Truth is not found in a book. — Truth is not to be found in a book. Furthermore, such a book merely presents a barrier to progress in your search for truth. Independent inquiry is needed in your search for truth, not dependence on anyone else's view or a mere book.

"A finger pointing to the moon." — These few paragraphs at best are merely "a finger pointing to the moon." Please do not take the finger to be the moon or fix your intense gaze on the finger and thus miss all the beautiful sight of heaven. After all, the usefulness of the finger is in pointing away from itself to the light that illumines finger and all.

Emptiness — the end. — I have to leave now, my friend. You have a long journey ahead of you, and you must travel light. From now on drop all your burden of preconceived conclusions behind, and "open" yourself to everything and everyone ahead. Remember, my friend, the usefulness of a cup is in its emptiness.

The end is the beginning. — The beginning and the end thus turn into next-door neighbors. On the musical scale, one may start with the lowest pitch and gradually ascend to the highest. When the highest is reached one finds it is located next to the lowest. To know, but to be as though not knowing, is the height of wisdom.

The aphorisms in this collection are cataloged by number, as follows, for cross-reference with other works in the Bruce Lee Library series.